Classical Education

The Movement Sweeping America

Gene Edward Veith, Jr.

& Andrew Kern

edited by Brian Phillips

Third Edition

CAPITAL RESEARCH CENTER
Washington, D.C.

Table of Contents

I

The Lost Content of Learning

> Humpty Dumpty sat on a wall,
> Humpty Dumpty had a great fall;
> All the king's horses and all the king's men
> Couldn't put Humpty together again.
> —*Mother Goose*

John Dewey (1859-1952) was the most important modernist education theorist; he believed it more important to teach the process of learning than the content of what was learned. For example, children should be taught how to read, not what to read—a theory that, like many works of modern art, divorced form and content. The words of Homer, Shakespeare, and Longfellow were unnecessary, because Dick, Jane, and Spot could teach reading just as efficiently.

At higher levels, the process approach to education taught children how to conduct experiments but neglected what scientists had already discovered. They were encouraged to create their own art, but not to appreciate great art. Skills were put in conflict with knowledge.

These modernist approaches cut back the role of the intellect by separating the process of learning, to which they devoted much attention, from the objects of knowledge, which they treated as provisional. Dewey's narrowly empirical and behavioralist approach to how we know ended up minimizing what can be known. It was decreed that education could no longer teach unchanging truths and ideals because our learning processes and skills could never know such things.

The Road to Postmodernism

In 1909, John Dewey delivered a lecture at Columbia University entitled, "The Influence of Darwin on Philosophy" in which he proclaimed that Charles Darwin's *Origin of Species* had invoked an "intellectual revolt and introduced a new intellectual temper."[1] He explained that

The conceptions that had reigned in the philosophy of nature and knowledge for two thousand years, the conceptions that had become the familiar furniture of the mind, rested on the assumption of the superiority of the fixed and final ... the *'Origin of Species'* introduced a mode of thinking that in the end was bound to transform the logic of knowledge, and hence the treatment of morals, politics, and religion.[2]

Dewey found Darwin's theory conducive to his own radical naturalism and used it to call for radical change in education. He claimed, "Old ideas give way slowly" and "intellectual progress usually occurs through sheer abandonment of questions .... We do not solve them: we get over them."[3]

Darwin, then, had given the world an excuse to "get over" the enduring questions and absolutes of morality, politics, and religion, exchanging them for the urgent interests of the day. Dewey applied his understanding of Darwin to American educational practice, which brought about an "intellectual revolt" against the classical tradition and its "intellectual temper" and its preference for the unchanging.

Dewey abandoned any claim to be able to know what was permanently good, true, and beautiful. He wanted students to learn rational and scientific methods so that they would be equipped to acquire what was useful to them, according to their own interests. Deluded by what he thought were the discoveries of the natural sciences operating apart from philosophy and theology, Dewey insisted on isolating the sciences still further. Now, going one step beyond, many philosophers of science say we can know nothing. Dewey, the modernist, opened the Pandora's box of postmodernism.

Modernism celebrated the physical sciences as the measure of all things. But postmodernism celebrates the social sciences because it regards man's will as the measure of all things. Modernists believed in the idea of objective truth, although they reduced truth to what can be measured by science. But postmodernists reject altogether the idea of objective truth. Postmodernists say that truth is really a "construction" of the mind or society. The meaning of everything is determined by the culture in which we live.

Postmodernism is also shaping the field of education, even though it undermines the very possibility of learning. If there is no objectively true content, what will there be to teach? If there are no intellectual standards, how can children be assessed? If there are no moral absolutes, how can children be disciplined and educated to be responsible citizens?

Postmodernism takes its toll not only on the learning of knowledge but also on the learning of skills. Although the process of inquiry can still be taught, postmodernism's distrust of language, social norms, and empirical reality makes it hardly worth the trouble. Students, for instance, can learn methods to cultivate their subjectivity and to explore and share their feelings. They can also be taught to establish new social and political identities as members of (usually victimized) groups. But processes such as learning how to read, write, and calculate are neglected in favor of such postmodern values as entertainment, group interaction, and consciousness-raising.

In this way postmodernism is really another name for relativism. Truth is relative. What is true for you may not be true for me. Morality is also relative. What a person considers "good" arises from his private choices and subjective "values," not from objective standards grounded in a transcendent religious law or a rational concept of the common good. "What is right for you may not be right for me." There are no absolutes in society: post-modernists like to say they "deconstruct" the traditional absolutes of truth, beauty, and goodness. To use another of their slogans, postmodernism is "anti-foundational," that is, there are no foundations upon which to build—not reason, revelation, tradition, or anything else.

Federal Intervention

Of course, buildings without foundations are bound to crumble, but the U.S. government has launched myriad federal interventions to prop up the educational system. Over the last half-century, the federal government has enacted onerous and rapidly changing legislation, all designed to "help" the failing school system. In the last 20 years the government has been particularly active.

In 1994, then President Bill Clinton signed into law "Goals 2000," a federal education initiative founded upon the principles of "outcomes-based" education that used standardized test scores and other "measurable" results to determine the success of students, teachers, schools, districts, and entire states.

Following the failure of "Goals 2000," President George W. Bush brought forth "No Child Left Behind" in 2001. This initiative evolved as it passed through Congress, but the eventual law retained the idea of "standards-based" testing, meaning students were evaluated against lists of what students needed to know to be "educated." Teacher training and curriculum development was also geared to the dissemination of those standards.

Like Goals 2000, No Child Left Behind would soon prove a disappointment and be replaced by yet another federal education initiative. In 2009, President Barack Obama authorized the massive "American Recovery and Reinvestment Act" which, among many other things, allocated $77 billion in direct funding for education ($30.8 billion towards "college affordability" and $33.6 billion for "school modernization"). Additionally, 2009 saw the appearance of the "Race to the Top" initiative, which financially rewarded schools for complying with upcoming "Common Core" standards. In dire financial straits, many states signed on to "Race to the Top" without knowing the effects or even the full content of Common Core.

In 2010, the Common Core Standards Initiative was unveiled. One of its primary goals was the elimination of separate state standards, to be replaced by nationally established ones. As criticism of Common Core has mounted, several states which initially adopted the standards have already filed repeal legislation.

The advancement of Common Core reveals a still greater problem in the American educational system, namely the glaring separation between responsibility and authority. Lawmakers, who approve the education initiatives, bear no responsibility when their measures fail. States and schools, however, are threatened with loss of funding and other resources if they do not live up to the federally established requirements.

Viruses of the Mind

The problems within the American educational system apparently cannot be repaired through legislation because they are systemic and philosophical; they are rooted in adherence to certain "viruses" of the mind. While it could be argued (quite successfully) that John Dewey was the conduit for the introduction of postmodern thought into schools, several other philosophies accompanied him. Among them were radical forms of empiricism, rationalism, and romanticism.

The ideas of empiricism found their clearest expression in Francis Bacon (1561-1626), the inventor of the "scientific method" which has also been called the "Baconian method." Expanding far beyond mere scientific inquiry, Bacon's approach was applied to all knowledge and gave rise to the idea that knowledge can only be derived from sense experience. John Locke (1632-1704), the father of British Empiricism, would even argue that man, at birth, is a *tabula rasa,* a blank slate, and gains knowledge only through sense experience.

If Francis Bacon is the "father of empiricism," then René Descartes (1596-1650) is the "father of rationalism." The Frenchman established his name as a brilliant thinker through his work in analytical geometry and physics, but he is perhaps most remembered for his strong appeal to "radical doubt" as the foundation for all knowledge. Adopting as his motto *De omnibus dubitandum* ("all things are to be doubted"), Descartes tried to establish a kind of first principle, the foundational principle upon which all knowledge could be built. In his *Meditations on First Philosophy,* he wrote: "I must once for all seriously undertake to rid myself of all the opinions which I had formerly accepted, and commence to build anew from the foundation if I wanted to establish any firm and permanent structure in the sciences." For Descartes, to know anything meant first to doubt everything.

Romanticism rose as a literary, artistic, and intellectual reaction against the increased industrialization and mechanism of the seventeenth and eighteenth centuries. Though the Romantic movement consisted of many still influential writers—among them, William Wordsworth, John Keats, Percy Shelley, and Samuel Taylor Coleridge—the most enduringly influential was also the most controversial, Jean-Jacques Rousseau (1712-1778). Born in Geneva, Rousseau was a largely self-educated philosopher and author who wrote extensively about human nature, politics, education, and more. He argued that man was naturally good and born free, enslaved only by society and its moral demands and trappings. As a result, man must be freed from such constraints and allowed to follow instead his emotions and natural feelings as the path to truth.

All these ideologies have collided with great force in the American educational system, apparently with little concern for the chaos of contradiction they produce. Now it seems that Francis Bacon runs the research, and thus the modern textbook companies; René Descartes runs the administration, thus standardized testing; and Jean-Jacques Rousseau runs the classroom, thus the relativistic morality and "child-centered" pedagogical approach. The end result is near-constant conflict between curriculum developers, school administrators, and teachers. The differing philosophies create an ideological war zone, with children caught in the "no man's land" between the trenches.

It seems that the only way to reconcile such variant ideas within a school system is to deny truth itself.

Multiculturalism

One trend in postmodernist education is the idea of "multiculturalism." With few exceptions, this cliché has little to do with actually studying or appreciating other cultures. Instead, it is a way to teach a kind of heavily politicized relativism. Postmodernists believe an individual's identity consists primarily of the qualities that make him a member of a group—a race or ethnicity, a gender, sexual preference, or some other collective identity. So multiculturalism starts out as a relativist assertion ("Every culture has different ideas and beliefs that are true for it"), then becomes a form of criticism ("What makes you think your way of thinking about this subject is superior to another culture's way?"), and finally becomes an attack on Western civilization and American society ("Your ideas about this subject reflect your upbringing in a culture that oppresses certain victim groups and gives power to certain oppressor groups").

A genuine comparison would reveal that cultures share universal elements: greatly different cultures may hold common attitudes toward love, family, sexual morality, and property. Further scholarly study would disclose that most non-Western cultures favor social practices that would embarrass or offend radical feminists, homosexual activists, or environmentalists. But multiculturalism is not scholarship. It is a latter-day romanticism—a particularly Western mode of thinking. Multiculturalism projects a nobility onto other cultures in order to denigrate the Western heritage. At the same time it is obsessed by the suspicion that behind every good intention in our society lies a disguised desire to oppress.

If culture's impact on the individual is so all encompassing, as postmodernists say, how is it possible to go beyond it? Why shouldn't we simply accept our culture's traditions without question? Classical education studies local traditions from the standpoint of universal human principles, and it appreciates the commonalities that people of all cultures share. Unlike advocates of multiculturalism, a classical educator does not urge women and minority students to submerge their personal and moral identities into the presumed character of their race, sex, or ethnicity. Oddly, multiculturalists never extend this invitation to the white, the male, or the American. Postmodernist multiculturalism—and our nation's classrooms—are torn by such inconsistencies and contradictions.

Postmodernist Pedagogy: Reading

Postmodernist teachers encourage students to cultivate their subjectivities and create their own personal meanings. In the words of a teachers' union publication:

> Each human being must inevitably develop or construct meaning. Learning is not a matter of merely reading, listening and repeating what others say is true. Each of us must "make meaning" or make sense of our own world.[4]

While there is a kernel of practical truth to this statement, its universal application to learning undercuts the objectivity of knowledge—and with it the expectation that one can learn from what others, past and present, have discovered.

On a practical level, postmodernist pedagogy encourages students to have a good time. Classroom activities that entertain (role-playing exercises, computer games, and watching videos) take priority over those that are challenging and demanding. Teachers are urged to avoid "value judgments" because grades, like other objective standards, are only subjective impressions. As long as students stay involved in projects, no matter what the projects' intellectual content may be, they are thought to benefit from the experience. If a lesson stimulates, it has "worked." Material that is not fun—higher-level math, theoretical science, difficult books, complex reasoning—is not emphasized.

University schools of education and state departments of public instruction actively encourage experimentation, but they make it extremely difficult to halt failed experiments. Indeed, the promotion and tenure system rewards curriculum designers, textbook authors, and education bureaucrats who sell "new ideas" and "cutting-edge" approaches to pedagogy. Many of the new ideas do not work, but once accepted in school curricula they are hard to remove.

Consider the teaching of reading. The genius of our alphabetic writing system, invented millennia ago by the Semitic peoples of the Middle East, is that it uses symbols for sounds. It is unlike the Chinese language, in which every word consists of a separate ideogram that may be pronounced differently in a variety of dialects. Our phonetic alphabet enables a person to read and write by learning only 26 symbols, not 50,000 ideograms. Because it is easier for common people to become literate in

English than in Chinese, it is not surprising that universal literacy—and democracy—spread fairly quickly through the West, unlike China, where knowledge and political power was restricted by a tiny, highly educated elite.

The traditional "phonics" method of teaching children to read builds on the strength of the 26-letter alphabet and has children "sound out" a word syllable by syllable, but in recent decades education experts have promoted a new way to learn reading. Children are taught to recognize the shape of the entire word. The experts say most experienced readers do not sound out words; they visually recognize the "whole word." Why can't new readers be taught to do the same? Certain educational psychologists contend that children learn differently: some are oriented to sounds, others to visual images. But "whole word" theorists assume most of today's TV generation are "visual learners." As a result, phonics is replaced with flash cards, complete with mnemonic devices to help children memorize the appearance of the "whole word" (the word "cat" might be given a little tail on the "t" and ears and whiskers on the "c").

"Whole word" (also called "see-say") advocates have devised a reading and writing program called "Whole Language." As a book on the subject explains: Reading is "a process of generating hypotheses in a meaning-making transaction in a socio-historical context." The post-modernist ideology is apparent: reading and writing are "not a matter of 'getting the meaning' from the text ... [but] a matter of readers using the cues print provides and knowledge they bring with them ... to construct a unique interpretation .... There is no single 'correct meaning' for a given text, only plausible meanings."[5] If there is no objective meaning in language, only constructions of unique interpretations, it would seem impossible to learn, understand, and communicate. University professors may receive tenure for such solipsistic theories, but it seems little short of lunacy to use them to teach first-graders.

Since the whole language method—with its notorious "creative spelling"—was adopted in elementary schools across the country, reading ability has plummeted. California's reading scores dropped to dead last after the state mandated the whole-language approach.[6] To be sure, many bright children can be taught to read by the whole-word method just as experienced readers quickly "attack" new words by unconsciously relating them to spoken language. But this approach handicaps children of average or below average ability. Most children can memorize only a limited number of word-shapes. And the method is of no help when they encounter new words. The whole-word method cannot work because it rejects our alphabetic system and turns words into ideograms. The English language might as well be Chinese.

In more recent days, another approach known as "balanced literacy" has risen to the fore. This approach combines several different types of reading techniques, from "reading workshops" in which students are directly taught the internal dialogue they should have while reading to "shared readings" in which students and teachers take turns reading from the same book and sharing their thoughts, from "guided readings" in which teachers ask students questions while they read to "independent readings" selected by the students. All of these occasions are followed by "sharing times" in which students are encouraged to share their thoughts about the text read. Critics of the "balanced literacy" approach have pointed out that it provides only a skill or method without encouraging comprehension. In that way, the balanced-literacy and whole-language approaches seem cut from the same cloth.

Postmodernism in education spells catastrophe. "Meaning-making" theories based on the premises of relativism cannot achieve the goals of education: knowledge, skills, the ability to reason, and the transfer of standards of moral character and good citizenship. The developmental psychologist Howard Gardner has said of postmodern theory, "Taken at face value, the postmodern stance invalidates my enterprise of creating an education that focuses on the true, the beautiful and the good."[7]

Progressivism

Given the failure of postmodernism in education, as well as the frustration caused by federal interventions and the attempts to blend the contradictory ideas of empiricism, rationalism, and romanticism, one is tempted to ask what could possibly hold the current educational system together at all? The answer is progressivism.

The essence of progressivism is the denial that the truth can be known. In this view, everything is in a state of constant change. When applied to education, this theory dictates that students are no longer be taught to know permanently true, good, and beautiful things because such things do not exist (at worst) or are simply unknowable (at best). Instead, the children are taught to adapt to their environment.

What's more, students are no longer taught the tools that have been developed to know the good, the true, and the beautiful. Because the possibility of knowable truth is denied, practical disciplines like phonics, times tables, drills, and memorization are removed, downplayed, and even seen as oppressive to a child's learning.

Progressive education has brought about the rise of the analytical or "hyper-scientific" mind, with a heavy emphasis on standardized tests and "measurable" results. What a student knows, his or her level of education, is easily reduced to a series of multiple-choice bubbles and Scan-tron sheets. No longer concerned with truth, progressive education enacts a disintegrated curriculum and promotes the specialization of learning, creating generations of "science nerds," "artsy people," and so on. Since there is no sense to make of anything, all learning becomes compartmentalized and segmented.

The primary trouble with the progressive approach is that it does not correspond to reality. What ought to disturb true progressivists is the way their pragmatic theories simply do not work. Where these theories have been applied, students do not learn how to read, their ability to pay attention is diminished, they fail to learn math (which, in turn, reduces their ability to contribute to the sciences), and they are generally disabled from participation in the civic life of a free people.

Progressive education creates a sense of helplessness and dependence, which is the opposite of freedom. It breeds ignorance that leads to vice, and vice that leads to the disintegration of culture. Such a result, however, should be expected because progressive thought is based upon a rejection of both nature and tradition. The rejection of nature leads to the denial of the human faculties that allow us to perceive truths. That is, because progressives deny the existence of knowable truth, even the faculties we have for perceiving truth—memory, attentiveness, logic, etc.—are undermined and left undeveloped. This causes progressives, in turn, to reject the conventions and traditions that developed and strengthened those faculties, such as phonics, drills, memorization, and times tables.

What Now?

Reformers have endorsed a variety of schooling alternatives to combat the decline of American education. Many policy proposals center on privatizing educational finance and governance. These proposals would use the incentives that would come from redirecting the flow of money to reform the education system. Advocates of "school choice" insist that public schools will improve if they have to compete for students and taxpayer dollars.

Market forces will spur innovation, reward good schools, and put bad schools out of business.

The effort to empower parents rather than government bureaucrats in education is certainly worthwhile, but the question of educational philosophy remains. Many private schools use the same modernist and post-modernist approaches to education that prevail in government-run schools. Even private schools with strong religious identities may use such flawed curricula, teacher training, and pedagogy. These religious schools may offer religious instruction and hold students to stricter standards of classroom discipline, but many still fail to teach students adequately.

Numerous attempts at educational reform simply reinforce the failings of the education establishment. Responding to the clamor for school improvement, many states have imposed stricter academic requirements on teachers. But forcing teachers to take even more education courses based on failed theories is not the answer.

After reaching so many dead-ends, a growing number of frustrated parents are turning to the most radical education reform: home-schooling. The ultimate in one-on-one instruction, home-schooling puts control of instruction and discipline directly into the hands of parents. Studies show that home-schooled children regularly exhibit high academic performance and benefit from close parental support. Yet even here contemporary education theories insinuate themselves. Some homeschoolers employ a "learning as play" curriculum which hardly justifies parents' investment of time and effort.

What homeschoolers, education policy reformers, concerned businesspeople, technophiles, and teachers and administrators in religious academies and government schools alike need is a different philosophy of education. Many are searching for new and innovative techniques. But a technique is only a means to an end. The real issue is the purpose of education.

The search for education alternatives is leading many homeschoolers, as well as private and public school parents and academic reformers, along a variety of paths to rediscover something singular and essential: classical education, the education that gave us Western civilization.

II

The Elements of Classical Education

Classical education cultivates wisdom and virtue by nourishing the soul on truth, goodness, and beauty. The ancient Greeks and Romans recognized that free citizens require an education that enlarges the mind and cultivates the soul. They believed that the cultivation of virtue, knowledge of the world and of human nature, active citizenship, and practical action all demand this purpose-driven education. When Christianity was planted in the soil of the classical world, its adherents found what was good and true in classical thought, purged out the dross, and handed on the rest to their heirs.

In recent decades, as the classical renewal in education has matured, we have sought to understand its nature and secrets and to discover its essential ingredients. This essay proposes four elements that define classical education and that provide the ground on which we must meet the coming trials:

1. A high view of man

2. Logocentrism

3. Responsibility for the Western tradition

4. A pedagogy that sustains these commitments

A High View of Man

In the heart of classical education beats the conviction that the human being is a creature of timeless significance. The Christian goes so far as to see him as the Image of God, the lord-steward of the creation on whose virtue the well-being of the earth and its inhabitants depends, and as a priest, offering the creation to God for the sake of its flourishing and his own blessedness.

The purpose of classical education, therefore, is to cultivate human excellence, or *virtue*, which is that word's original meaning.

Yet this high view of man is no self-indulgent fantasy, for it carries with it the duty to strive for nobility that the classical educator perceives in every person. Human flourishing depends, not on one's material well-being or adjustment to society, but on one's relation to the true, the good, and the beautiful.

In *Norms and Nobility*, David Hicks argues that a fully rendered image of man includes three domains: the social, the individual, and the religious. Educators, then, must envision students' engagement in their communities, both as voters and as leaders. Educators must also recognize that students have their own spiritual lives on which their citizenship and their economic life depend. A wise and virtuous citizenry not only supports the economy through entrepreneurship and innovation, it also challenges the powerful with well-reasoned arguments rooted in a love for liberty and virtue. A classical education cultivates the creativity and spiritual lives of students so that the much-celebrated (and much neglected) "whole child" is truly prepared for real life, without losing touch with his deepest and most intimate self. Thus are all three dimensions honored, and society benefits from the membership and quiet influence of well-rounded, healthy persons.

According to the classical tradition, the true, the good, and the beautiful are the soul's nourishment. Furthermore, as Image of God, a person is able to know them. To fulfill this role, a person's human faculties to perceive truth, to love and reproduce the beautiful, and to revere and act on the good must be cultivated. A faculty refined to a pitch of excellence becomes a virtue, such as wisdom or kindness. Christian classical education cultivates the human capacity to know and act on this holy triumvirate, thus nurturing wise and virtuous souls.

Furthermore, the classical educator lives in a knowable and harmonious cosmos that makes ultimate sense. A system can make sense only if it possesses a unifying principle, or "Logos." Without such a logos, true knowledge is impossible.

Logocentrism

Christians recognize that Christ is that Logos. He makes reason possible, harmonizes everything, and creates the conditions for ordered, knowable truth. He is the unifying principle of thought, the key in which the music of the spheres is played, the archetype of every virtue.

The commitment to a logos that makes ultimate sense of the cosmos and makes knowledge possible is expressed in the much-maligned word, "Logocentrism." According to a logocentric view of the universe, organized knowledge can be discovered, arranged, and even taught. This is the first principle of the Christian classical curriculum.

As everything is ordered by a logos, so each particular thing has its own logos, or nature—in Latin, *species.* The power to see truth is the ability to see the nature of particular things and to see each of them in their relations to each other. The tools of learning enable a learner to identify the nature of a thing and to relate to that thing in a manner suited to its nature. Without this knowledge, a human cannot bless what he is interacting with, whether it be a horse, a farm, or a child's soul.

Perceiving that humans live in a cosmos that makes ultimate sense and that they share it with other members of that cosmos, each of which can be known according to their natures, the Christian classical educator is reminded of his responsibility as a steward and priest. The knowledge available to us is not given to amass power, but to cultivate and guard the earth. The whole creation groans and travails when creation's lord shirks his stewardship of stewardship.

Responsibility for the Western Tradition

Classical educators take responsibility for Western civilization. The West is unique in its view of mankind as the Image of a transcendent God and in its acceptance of the view that both truth and the world can be known. These commitments are the hinges for much that defines Western civilization.

Western civilization is the property of all who live in America. Our national roots have grown deep in the customs, traditions, discoveries, and conversations that make up American, British, European, Greek, Roman, and Hebrew history. It is our privilege to receive and to share this heritage, and it is just as immoral to keep it from others as it is to despise our heritage.

Christ formulated the essential political doctrine of the West: "You shall know the truth, and the truth shall set you free." But this idea permeated Western thought from the time when Moses freed the Israelites from their Pharaoh-worshipping masters and when Aristotle developed his politics and ethics.

Truth alone, the tradition insists, can sustain the political ideals of liberty and human rights. If the truth cannot be known and does not govern human societies, then there is nothing to restrain the rulers. If rights are not derived from truth, then they are granted by the ever-changing state. Liberty and knowable truth are interdependent.

Because truth is needed to be healthy and free, classical educators believe that to empower the powerless, prepare students for a job, and enable future citizens to play their role in society, every child needs a classical education: deliberate training in perceiving the true, the good, and the beautiful through the tools of learning.

The classical educator understands that Western civilization is as full of vice as it is of virtue. He does not "privilege" or even idealize Western civilization; he assumes responsibility for it. While the conventional educator seems to see Western civilization as something to escape, the classical educator sees it as the locus of his vocation.

He demands a conversation that challenges his culture and himself with the standards of the true, the good, and the beautiful. He understands that survival and power are not their own justifications. Agreeing with the oracle that, "The unexamined life is not worth living," he continues the Western habit of perpetual self-examination.

He appreciates that the Western tradition contains elements of restless idealism, non-conformity, and self-examination. These have always threatened the status quo while also revealing new springs of cultural nourishment. One of the goals of classical education is to discern the appropriate manner by which the mistreated and oppressed can challenge their oppressors without destroying their civilization.

While the classical educator recognizes the West's recent achievements, especially in technology, he fears that, having lost its moorings in knowable truth, the West has become deaf to challenges from within its own tradition. The modern West, to the classical educator, is the prodigal son, energetically spending his inheritance, perhaps far from "coming to himself."

Nevertheless, while the classical educator may agree with those who contend that the West is in decline, his sense of responsibility prohibits despair. Instead, he diagnoses the decline as the loss of confidence in the true, the good, and the beautiful, and offers a cure in the renewed quest for that truth, goodness, and beauty. To this end, he offers a classical education.

An Appropriate Pedagogy

Western civilization, the classical educator believes, offers its children a rich heritage on which they can feed their own souls and those of their neighbors. The classical curriculum provides the means to do so.

The classical curriculum can be divided into two stages. First, the student masters the arts of learning. Then he uses the skills and tools mastered to enter the great conversation, which is another way to say, to study the sciences.

The classical curriculum begins with an apprenticeship in what has come to be known as the "tools of learning," a term coined by Aristotle when he developed his elementary handbooks. He called them *The Organon,* which is Greek for "tool." *The Organon* provided the foundation of the trivium in the medieval school and was combined with the quadrivium to form the seven liberal arts.

These arts of learning give the classical curriculum its form. Those who master them gain access to a realm of unified knowledge that includes the natural and moral sciences, philosophy, and theology.

The seven liberal arts are not subjects per se, nor do they compose a "general education." Instead, they are the arts of learning that enable one to move from subject to subject, text to text, or idea to idea, knowing how to handle the particular subject, text, or idea. More than that, they introduce the student to the arts and convictions needed for a community and its members to remain free. They are the trunk of the tree of learning, on which the various sciences are branches.

Probably the term with which classical education is most closely associated in the popular mind is the word *trivium,* which is a paradigm for the mastery of language. The Latin *trivium* literally means "where three roads meet," and it refers to grammar, logic, and rhetoric. But the *trivium* applies to far more than language. To be educated in any discipline, you must (1) know its basic facts (grammar); (2) be able to reason clearly about it (logic); and (3) communicate its ideas and apply it effectively (rhetoric). Nevertheless, the trivium of grammar, logic, and rhetoric is fundamentally a collection of language arts.

The priority the classical educator places on language turns his attention to the classical languages: Latin and Greek. Tracy Lee Simmons proposes in *Climbing Parnassus* that classical education is "a curriculum grounded upon ... Greek, Latin and the study of the civilization from which they arose." Ravi Jain and Kevin Clarke add, "The indispensability of the study of classical languages ... is something that our schools will have to realize if they desire faithfully to remain in the classical tradition."

Classical educators defend Latin and Greek in a number of ways. They are convinced that language studies discipline the mind. Nothing cultivates attentiveness, memory, precision of thought, the ability to think in principles, communication, and overall accuracy like the study of Latin and Greek.

In addition, Greek and Latin authors recorded an astounding range and depth of political thought from a wider perspective over a longer period of time and covering a wider geography than is embodied in any other language. In the study of literature, Shakespeare, Chaucer, and Milton become isolated from their sources when the student encounters a language barrier between himself and Virgil, Ovid, or Homer. Most theology has been recorded in, and the church has sung its hymns in, Latin and Greek from the time of the apostles and the first martyrs.

The Great Conversation that is the beating heart of Western civilization took place in Latin and Greek and their offspring. A Western community lacking citizens versed in Latin and Greek must lose its heritage. The citizenry will communicate, vote, work, and think in a manner increasingly isolated from the sources of their own identity. For those who love their heritage and who want to offer the riches of that heritage to others, the classical languages are the *sine qua non*. As Alexis de Tocqueville wrote in his classic *Democracy in America*, "All who aspire to literary excellence in democratic nations ought frequently to refresh themselves at the springs of ancient literature; there is no more wholesome medicine for the mind."

The Quadrivium

Reality is linguistic. It is also mathematical. That is why the classical tradition emphasizes the quadrivium, the four liberal arts of arithmetic, geometry, music, and astronomy. These arts were related to mathematics because they dealt with numbers considered under different aspects.

Jain and Clarke have made an eloquent case for the quadrivium and the powers of the four mathematical arts. The ancients believed "that arithmetic led the soul from wonder to wisdom." Euclidian geometry "provides the paradigm of certain and airtight reasoning." Astronomy, the centerpiece of ancient science and the key to profound mysteries, gave birth to modern science. Music, surprisingly to the modern, was a driver of the scientific revolution. "It may," say Clarke and Jain, "be the chief art of the quadrivium." Until very recently, a man could not claim to be well-educated until he had mastered the quadrivium.

Classical educators see the arts of the quadrivium as essential tools that enable us to perceive the reality of the world around us and our relation to it. They also discipline and open the mind. Therefore, say Jain and Clarke, "Classical schools must uphold a high standard for mathematical education precisely for its special role in human formation and developing the virtue of the mind."

It is important to remember, however, that the trivium and quadrivium are not discrete subjects. They are modes of learning. Nor are they ends in themselves. They are tools for learning. The thing learned is knowledge, for which the Latin word is *scientia,* or science. A science, then, is a domain of knowing.

To the classical educator, the word *science* is much more inclusive than its conventional use. While the modern usually thinks of science as natural science, the classical educator recognizes that there are other kinds of knowledge, much more practical, though less precise, than natural science. These include the moral sciences (history, ethics, politics, etc.), philosophy, and theology.

Natural science deals with knowledge of the material world. Moral science considers human flourishing and is driven by the question: "How is virtue cultivated in the soul and in community?" Philosophical science explores first causes and theories of knowledge. Theological science is the knowledge of God and His revelation. Each science gains its own kind of knowledge, responding to its own set of inquiries and developing its own tools to gain the kind of knowledge it seeks.

The experimentation and calculation used in the natural sciences can contribute to discussions over ethical matters, but these tools are not adequate to answer either the daily questions that make up human life or the large socio-political issues that determine the destinies of human society. For this, what Socrates called "dialectic," and what has come to be called the great conversation, is necessary.

Russell Kirk argued that, "The end of liberal education is the disciplining of free minds." The means to that end is the great conversation, an exploration of the human soul and the quest for the best way to live the truth in present circumstances. It draws the students' attention to soul-fortifying ideas that reflect permanently relevant truths. Contemplating the great books and great works of art draws the student out of himself and his own age into those permanent and powerful tools for living and to the truths that transcend the practical.

The classical curriculum is a formidable and comprehensive theory of education. It is one of the great creations of Western thought. By mastering the tools of the seven liberal arts and participating in the great conversation, the student is nourished in all his faculties and equipped for the never-ending battle (internal and external) for liberty rooted in truth, where virtue can be cultivated and beauty can be incarnated in art, action, custom, and thought.

In closing it must be added that this course cannot be properly run if the pedagogy does not match it in goal and means. Only dialectical engagement with the truth can lead to the soul's apprehension of that truth. Only a true apprenticeship in the tools of truth-seeking can set a person free. There can be no guarantees.

Can classical education be adapted to the needs and culture of the twenty-first century? Yes, it can. It is neither of one time nor one culture, but is grounded in human nature and in the nature of learning. Classical education offers an intellectual framework that is disciplined and liberating, open both to the past and to new knowledge.

III

Christian Classicism

Classical education has always been nourished by the Christian Church. The Christian scholar Boethius (c. 480–524) first divided the seven liberal arts into the trivium and quadrivium as part of the early Church's endeavor to understand the relationship between Greco-Roman civilization and Christianity. The medieval university, which was organized around the liberal arts, was likewise a creation of the Church. The Protestant Reformation, which proclaimed that lay Christians must read the Bible, championed universal education. Protestant churches opened thousands of schools in the Old and New Worlds, which nearly always followed the classical model.

As we shall see, parochial education even today retains elements of classical education. Many Catholic schools still model their curricula on the medieval education archetype, some more consciously and with greater rigor than others. A number of Lutheran parochial schools are also returning to their classical roots. Certainly the catechetical model of religious education as practiced in Catholic, Lutheran, and Reformed traditions is grounded in the classical method: children memorize creeds and prayers (grammar); they work through the catechism, which is written as a dialectical exchange of questions and answers (logic); then they make their own profession of faith at Confirmation (rhetoric).

Recently, aroused by the hostile secularization of public education, Christians have been opening their own schools in droves. Even churches that have not had a tradition of parochial education are establishing Christian schools, as are groups of concerned parents and alliances of cultural conservatives. Some of these schools seem more dedicated to insulating children from the temptations of the world than to offering them a comprehensive education. But other Christian schools are rediscovering their rich educational heritage, and these have become major catalysts for the classical revival.

The Association of Classical and Christian Schools

Douglas Wilson is the Senior Minister of Christ Church in Moscow, Idaho. Wilson says that the birth of his first daughter was the cause of the Association of Classical and Christian Schools. Dismayed at the state of contemporary education, Wilson promised his wife that when their daughter was ready for kindergarten they would be ready to give her an education that was worthy of their beliefs.

Wilson's thinking was strongly influenced by a 1947 essay he read by the English scholar and novelist Dorothy L. Sayers, known both for the "Lord Peter Wimsey" mysteries and her translations of Dante. That essay, "The Lost Tools of Learning," is a lucid explanation of the trivium and the liberal arts tradition. Sayers ended her essay, however, with a lament that the trivium was unlikely to be used in modern times to educate children. Wilson, who was a classics major as an undergraduate, resolved in this one detail to prove her wrong; he decided that his daughter's future supplied more than sufficient reason to establish a school organized on the principles that Sayers' essay outlined.

Logos School opened its doors in 1980. It had 19 students. By the 2011-12 school year Logos had grown to 355 students, offering a comprehensive kindergarten through high school curriculum. Wilson's gift to his daughter was the pilot school that launched an international education movement.

Wilson's experience at Logos led him in 1991 to write a book that lays out his ideas. It pays homage to Sayers' essay in the title: *Recovering the Lost Tools of Learning: An Approach To Distinctively Christian Education.* The book struck a nerve in the American Christian community, and it has spurred the creation of a host of schools organized on the Logos model. In the summer of 1993, Logos School hosted a conference to explain the principles of classical education to representatives of new Christian schools and to train new teachers in its method. The schools went on to organize the Association of Classical and Christian Schools (ACCS). ACCS staff helps mount an annual conference that attracts up to 950 people annually, and its education seminars have trained hundreds of teachers in the ACCS approach to classical education.

When the first edition of this book was published in 1997, we wrote that ACCS had 56 member schools. By summer 2011, that number had grown to 229 schools, with over 34,000 students. They include Regents School of Austin, Texas; Veritas Academy of Lancaster County, Pennsylvania; Schaeffer Academy of Rochester, Minnesota; Cair Paravel Latin School of Topeka, Kansas; Ambrose School of Boise, Idaho; and The Oaks of Spokane, Washington. While the economic downturn slowed the number of new schools opening, the number of students continues to rise, with over 40,000 in the 2013-2014 school year attending 236 schools.

ACCS has also gained considerable global influence. Director of Accreditation Patch Blakey reported that calls come from around the world for the establishment of classical and Christian schools. Dr. George Grant, a regular speaker at ACCS conferences and founder of ACCS-affiliated Franklin Classical School, said, "We now have three thriving schools in Northern Iraq, twenty-seven in Indonesia, two in Egypt, one in Jordan, and many more in the planning stages." The three schools in Northern Iraq, The Classical Schools of the Medes, were planted through the cooperative efforts of Servant Group International along with local officials and community leaders, and have grown to nurture more than 1,500 students, over 95 percent of whom come from Kurdish Muslim families.

Yet ACCS has influenced more than the K-12 day schools that have joined the association: nine colleges have been granted membership or associate status, nearly fifty businesses and other affiliate members are included, and a number of homeschooling families and individuals. Curriculum developers such as Veritas Press and consultants like Better Schools have formed to support these many ventures.

Even given this growth, Blakey regards it as having only reached toddlerhood. Because of parental demand for information on the benefits of classical education, ACCS continues to promote the vision and to provide support for classical and Christian educators at its annual summer conference; through *Classis,* its bimonthly newsletter; through radio interviews; and through various electronic means such as the ACCS website, e-mail blasts, Facebook, Twitter, and the ACCS blog, "About Classical Education." In addition, ACCS invests considerable time in personal communications through e-mail and telephone calls. The result of all these activities is a flourishing movement of classical and Christian educators throughout the United States and in some surprising overseas locations.

ACCS began to accredit schools in 2000. As of this writing, they have accredited 32 member schools, with an additional 13 candidates working toward accreditation. To maintain ACCS accreditation, a school must implement an ACCS-approved teacher certification program, which helps schools maintain high-caliber classical instruction. To ensure that ACCS students are performing at a high level, the ACCS board recommends and promotes the ERB CTP-4 standardized test, which is widely used in the best private schools, and thus ensures a higher standard of assessment than the SAT or ACT.

The Theory

The signature of the ACCS school is its dedication to Dorothy Sayers' understanding of the trivium. According to Sayers' essay, the trivium's significance rests on three enduring factors: the need to accumulate tools for learning, the process by which any subject can be learned, and the developmental stages of a child's growth.

Sayers asked, "Is it not the great defect of our education today that although we often succeed in teaching our pupils 'subjects,' we fail lamentably on the whole in teaching them how to think?" She explained that the elements of the trivium—grammar, logic, and rhetoric—are not subjects; they are tools of thinking.

Sayers observed that the medieval school taught the trivium in order "to teach the pupil the proper use of the tools of learning before he began to apply them to 'subjects' at all." She explained that students in medieval schools first learned the grammar of a language and then were instructed in dialectic, i.e., they were taught to use language by defining terms, constructing an argument, and detecting logical fallacies. Finally, they learned to express themselves elegantly and persuasively. Specific subjects— the quadrivium—were taught only after students had shown they could master the tools of learning.

For Sayers, the power of the trivium was found in its progression and completeness. To this Sayers added her own progressive insight that the sequence of the trivium complements human development: its three component parts correspond to three stages in a child's growth.

Sayers argued that children at ages five to 11 in the primary grades are best suited to learn at the level of grammar. Just as young children can easily learn their own language, so can they acquire the most basic knowledge: learning how to write letters and sound out words, memorize the multiplication table, and listen to the classic stories of their country and culture. This is the province of what even today are often called "grammar schools."

By the time they have reached middle school, children aged 12 to 14 bare tormenting their parents by talking back, questioning authority, and acting "smart." But the impertinence and rebellion of early adolescence is actually a sign of minds that are prepared for learning's next phase: the questioning and probing that constitute logic.

At ages 15 to 18 teenagers are in high school. While they are growing more self-absorbed, they are also anxious to reach out to their peers. Strong emotions, romantic idealisms, and questions of personal identity well up in adolescents who yearn to be understood. This is the age for self-expression, for the art of communication that is rhetoric.

ACCS schools apply Sayers' insight by recognizing that the child, as he passes through these ages, requires a different pedagogy that is appropriate to his level of development as well as appreciative of his individuality. While the trivium is taught to all, its particular approach changes as the child changes. Moreover, students benefit because their education has a sequential and cumulative power as they move from the mode of grammar to that of logic, and then from logic to rhetoric.

The Faith Factor

Members of the Association of Classical and Christian Schools are not only classical in their methods; they are Christian in their faith. While much of the ACCS theory of education can be traced to the Greek and Latin authors of classical antiquity, all knowledge for these schools finds integration in the Christian worldview. Unlike the postmodernists, ACCS schools are grounded in the belief that truth is not only knowable and necessary, but also revealed.

Because we must seek the truth in order to know it, it becomes tremendously important to develop the right learning skills. These are necessarily rational skills such as logic, precise speech, reading, writing, and mathematics. ACCS schools insist on the centrality of God, who has revealed Himself in the language of the Bible and the facts of creation, and who provides the very grounds of education.

Besides the trivium, another element of classical education in the ACCS approach is a respect for the past. "An essential part of the classical mind is awareness of, and gratitude for, the heritage of western civilization," Wilson writes. He goes on to insist, "A classicist is not someone who agrees with anyone who has been dead two hundred years and whose books are still in print. But a classicist is a participant in what Mortimer Adler calls the 'great conversation.'"

Wilson advocates no Christian ghetto. He insists that the Christian must participate in this conversation to avoid "chronological parochial-ism"—the inability to stand outside one's own time and to consider the world from another point of view. "The refusal to learn from the past is suicidal," he says. "It destroys the individualism it seeks to glorify."

Students who are immersed in the great unfolding conversation of the ages will be transformed. Wilson recalls the words of Russell Kirk on the consequences of a classical education: "Being educated they will know that they do not know everything; and that there exist objects in life besides power, and money, and sensual gratification; they will take long views; they will look backward to ancestors and forward to posterity. For them education will not terminate on commencement day."

The study of Latin is yet another mark of classicism in ACCS schools. "Because we are engaging in a conversation with the past, the first order of business is to learn the language," says Wilson. He goes on to describe "practical" reasons for studying the ancient language, including increased competence in English, an appreciation for literature, an understanding of the infancy of Western civilization, practice in the analytic method, and providing a foundation for the study of modern languages. He argues that the very process of learning Latin, with its complex conjugations and declensions, requires mental gymnastics that strengthen the mind.

Christian Kopff, author of *The Devil Knows Latin: Why America Needs the Classical Tradition,* argues forcefully that, "The abolition of Latin and Greek effectively severed an entire culture from the stories that constituted … its mental infrastructure." That serious English discourse depends heavily on Greek and Latin is sufficient reason to study the classical languages, he insists. But there is a still more important reason. "Studying the ancient tongues allows us to hear our ancestors talking and thinking .... These are lines of communication we need to keep open," because "the past is our most important source of creativity."

The Practice

While students in an ACCS school study logic, Latin, and religion, they also take most of the courses that students take in other schools—history, math, science, and English. But it is not any particular class that is the mark of an ACCS education; rather, an ACCS education is distinct because it relies on the trivium as an approach to learning while cultivating a Christian outlook on the world. These have a profound impact on the organization and content of courses in ACCS schools.

At the "grammar school" level, children learn to read using phonics, they master arithmetic drills, and they begin Latin by memorizing vocabulary and inflectional endings. Memory is the key to all learning, a fact most obvious at this grammar level, one so well understood by the ancient Greeks that they gave the name Mnemosyne ("memory") to the mother of the Muses, who were the goddesses of learning. Memorizing lays the foundation for knowledge because it helps students accumulate a basic vocabulary of information and lore that they will learn to understand more deeply when they are older.

Modern education theorists tend to denigrate memorization, arguing that facts without understanding are useless. But although learning by rote is a lower order intellectual skill (grammar), it is suitable, and delightful, to seven- and eight-year-olds, whose capacity to independently understand (logic) or discuss (rhetoric) is limited—as any visit to an elementary school "sharing time" makes clear. The failure of the impatient modern educator to fill grammar stage children's memory robs these very children of much that they could understand when they reach the logic years.

Moreover, young children seem to enjoy learning this way: they take pride in their accomplishments and become confident in their powers. Mnemonic devices—songs, chants, tricks, recitations, and drills—assume the dimensions of a vast game. Visitors to ACCS schools soon discover that children are capable of prodigious feats of memory. Eight-year-old Latin scholars yell out verb endings at top speed. Third graders in Logos School social studies class will name the states in the Union and their capitals, and will recite three interesting facts about each one. For "Pi Day" (3/14) at Veritas Academy in Lancaster, Pennsylvania, a student memorized 400 digits of the mathematical constant pi, *just for the challenge.*

Though the ACCS offers participating schools some common curriculum, such as Latin primers and symbolic logic texts, member schools are also free to adopt existing resources. Teachers at the Geneva School in Orlando, Florida, happened upon the "Shurley Method," which teaches English grammar through the use of simple songs and chants that apply linguistic paradigms to any sentence. Devised by a public school English teacher, a Mrs. Shurley who systematized her methods into an extensive language arts curriculum, this approach has been widely adopted in ACCS schools. With the Shurley method, second graders parse sentences—identifying parts of speech, finding subjects and verbs, and analyzing sentence structure—with astonishing facility. ("Dogs bark. What barks? Dogs. Subject noun. What is said about dogs? Dogs bark. Active verb.").

Mathematics is often taught using the textbooks of John Saxon, the renegade educator whose use of drills, systematic repetition of basic operations, and cumulative learning has frequently improved standardized test scores where his methods have been tried. However, some ACCS schools have begun to question the validity of the Saxon method, and other classical educators are going back to the "old math" that demanded rigorous and creative problem-solving skills.

Reading is taught through literature, with a concentration on the classics. Some ACCS schools use the old literature-rich McGuffey's Readers. As soon as possible, however, young classical scholars are reading complete works. ACCS schools typically develop elaborate reading lists, ranging from *The Chronicles of Narnia* for younger children to *Moby Dick* for teenagers in high school, and include the classic works of Homer, Shakespeare, and Milton, as well as modern writers such as George Orwell and Flannery O'Connor.

The art curriculum at Orlando's Geneva School is based not on finger painting, coloring, or cutting pictures out of magazines, but on learning how to draw. First graders learn how to copy illustrations, an application of the classical technique of *imitatio* (developing skills by imitating works of the masters). Second graders develop aesthetic literacy by studying art history. By the fifth grade, children are drawing landscapes with a clear sense of perspective.

The nineteenth-century art critic and scholar John Ruskin insisted that learning to draw is an intellectual and even moral discipline because it develops habits of careful observation, accuracy, and appreciation for the beauty and structure of the external world. Geneva's art curriculum acknowledges this dictum. Does training in accurate drawing instead of anything-goes self-expression inhibit creativity? ACCS schools believe the discipline of drawing yields genuine art by laying the firm foundation for a personal aesthetic vision that will come into focus during the rhetoric stage of the child's development. Indeed, classical education consistently follows the principle that discipline does not inhibit creativity or freedom; on the contrary, it enables them.

As children move into early adolescence, they should be solidly grounded in the grammatical stage of their education. Now they are ready for the logical or dialectical phase of the trivium, and their middle school classes in literature, science, history, and math emphasize thinking and comprehension. Every course at this level is approached dialectically. At the

Geneva school, classrooms contain not only desks for tests and note-taking, but also "dens" of couches and stuffed chairs around low tables to encourage the give-and-take dialogue of Socratic dialectic.

The capstone of the dialectic stage is a formal course in logic. Eighth-graders learn to recognize logical fallacies and to construct valid syllogisms. They also delve into the complexities of symbolic logic, learning about categorical and truth-functional statements, constructing truth tables, and manipulating the math-like symbols of the 256 possible syllogisms, only twenty-four of which are valid. Logic, however, is not studied only abstractly. Verbal arguments are translated into propositional symbols and evaluated. In Orlando, a teacher plays a tape-recording of an abstruse theological debate and the class uses its training to assess the arguments and declare a winner. Not bad for junior high.

Students in high school move on to the rhetoric stage, where the emphasis is on graceful expression, independent thought, creativity, and originality. The mode of teaching shifts: from an emphasis on lecture and drill (grammar), to argument and questioning (logic), to open discussion of differing opinions. Class activities include debates, mock trials, individual presentations, and lots of writing. At The Regents School of Austin, students gather around one of five specially designed Harkness tables to participate in Socratic discussions.

Once again, a capstone course embodies the intent of the trivium at this level. Logos school requires a course in rhetoric that goes far beyond English composition. The author of its textbook is Aristotle. Students discuss the types of discourse, the parts of an argument, and the variety of rhetorical appeals. Works by Cicero and other master rhetoricians, old and new, complement Aristotle's treatise on rhetoric. Through original writing, students put the techniques into practice.

For the culminating project of the senior year, students research and write two papers, each 25–30 pages in length, on topics of their own choosing. The first is meant for an impartial audience, the second must be addressed to a hostile audience. Students then present—and defend—their papers before faculty panels. At the second oral examination, faculty members act as hostile readers. The student must refute their criticisms and vindicate his thesis. The process is less an exam than an intellectual rite of passage.

Is the ACCS approach effective? Hard data is difficult to come by. Because the trivium is developmental and cumulative, a student must pass from childhood to adulthood under its tutelage before its full effect can be known. Since the ACCS was not organized until 1993, most of the schools are still young and have turned out relatively few graduates. Moreover, most students in ACCS programs have come from other schools and entered classes at varying levels, which means that some students have little or no exposure to dialectic or even to rhetoric.

But the ACCS prototype, Logos School, has existed since 1980, and a number of its students have graduated from the entire sequence, including Douglas Wilson's daughter, the cause of it all. By all available measurements, the ACCS program is an astonishing success. On standardized achievement tests, three out of four Logos students consistently score in the top 25 percent. One class of Logos seniors had a composite—that is, an average—SAT score in the ninety-sixth percentile, meaning that the entire class ranked in the top 4 percent of students in the nation. In 2011-2012 six of 27 Logos juniors received letters of commendation and three were recognized as National Merit Semi-finalists. Logos students regularly outperform their peers in statewide academic contests. For instance, Logos has won the Idaho State Law Foundation's Mock Trial competition in 2010, 2011, and 2012 (with fourteen titles since 1995). The main problem for Logos graduates seems to be the intellectual let-down when they go to college.

As a college English professor, co-author Gene Edward Veith visited Logos School and spoke informally with its students. He read their papers and came away asking himself, "These are high school students?" They seemed far more accomplished than most of his college students. College seniors sometimes must write one senior paper, but these high school seniors write two, and they are more rigorously reviewed. Freshmen in college composition courses can barely write a thesis statement, but here are students who employ the *exordium and narratio* with style and grace, with well-supported arguments (thanks to that junior high school course in logic), and nary a comma out of place (the grammar school language training). The Logos students were poised, thoughtful, and interesting, concerned about the world and ready to take their place in it. Such are the benefits of a classical education.

IV

Democratic Classicism

> The Democratic promise of equal educational opportunity, half-fulfilled, is worse than a promise broken. It is an ideal betrayed.
> —Mortimer Adler, *The Paideia Proposal*

The two men most responsible for the revival of classical education in this century were Robert Maynard Hutchins, president of the University of Chicago from 1929 to 1951, and Mortimer Adler, leader of the Paideia movement. Hutchins' academic reforms and curricular innovations served as prototypes for colleges that wanted to provide a genuine liberal arts education. For Hutchins, classical education was no elitist affectation of the upper classes. Rather, the liberal arts—taught by "The Great Books" of all ages—would offer precisely the kind of education necessary to a democracy. Every citizen, he believed, needed to be equipped with the intellectual tools for self-government, personal success, and—in the original sense of the "liberal arts"—freedom.

Hutchins' approach for colleges and universities is also applicable to primary and secondary education. This has been a project of the philosopher Mortimer Adler, perhaps Hutchins' most productive associate, who, with the Paideia Group, developed an educational manifesto, *The Paideia Proposal.* Two years after Adler wrote *The Paideia Proposal,* he and his colleagues completed an accompanying educational syllabus, *The Paideia Program.* The Paideia Group wrote the essays in the *The Paideia Program* as suggestions to help teachers implement *The Paideia Proposal'*s precepts and recommendations in primary and secondary schools across America. Paideia is a call for radical educational reform in American public schools.

There are significant differences between schools that follow the Association of Classical Christian Schools (ACCS) and Paideia models.[1] ACCS questions the validity of government-run schooling; by contrast,

Adler wrote *The Paideia Proposal* to reform public schooling. Religion is foundational to the ACCS curriculum, and Christianity is the point of integration through which all knowledge is made complete. *The Paideia Proposal* does not dismiss the importance of religion, but its approach is more secular, and its foundational principle is democracy.[2] If the approach of ACCS can be described as Christian classicism, then the approach of *The Paideia Proposal* can best be described as democratic classicism.

Paideia educators tend to avoid the term "classicism" because, says Adler, it "names the arid and empty formalism which dominated education at the end of the last century. It emphasized the study of the classics for historical or philological reasons. It was interested in the past for the past's sake. It mistook drill for discipline."[3] Adler adds, "Our program is not a return to the classics as that word is so often taken to mean, simply going back to Greek and Roman antiquities. We are concerned with classics where the classics mean anything of enduring value."[4]

Nevertheless, Paideia is indeed a classical movement. None of the classical educational reforms we present in this book are exercises in mere antiquarianism. On the dedication page of *The Paideia Proposal*, Adler defines Paideia: "P A I D E I A (py-dee-a) from Greek, *pais, paidos*: the upbringing of a child (Related to pedagogy and pediatrics). In an extended sense, the equivalent of the Latin *humanitas* (from which "the humanities"), signifying the general learning that should be the possession of all human beings." Paideia's theory of education, and its practice of reading great books and discussing them in Socratic seminars, are eminently classical.

As Geraldine Van Doren explains in her introduction to a collection of Adler's essays, "Paideia is the culmination of Adler's lifelong, intense, loving, and often brutal struggle against the forces of utilitarianism, elitism, scientism, specialism, and any other dogma infesting American education."[5] This struggle and its various controversies in the field of education illustrate an important chapter in America's intellectual history. For more than 70 years Mortimer Adler fought what often seemed a losing battle for a liberal arts education. Resisting the conventional wisdom of an age dominated by positivist and pragmatist models of learning, Hutchins and Adler fought for the renaissance of classical education in American public schools. Paideia was born to be, and continues to be, a crusade for democratic classicism.

Mortimer Adler

Mortimer Adler taught at the University of Chicago from 1930 to 1952. He was an editor of *The Encyclopedia Britannica*, that magisterial modern example of the integration of knowledge, and he has written some 50 books, most of which aim to popularize knowledge of classical philosophy and demonstrate its moral and intellectual application to daily life. They include *How to Read a Book, Aristotle for Everybody, The Difference of Man and the Difference It Makes*, and *Six Great Ideas: Truth, Goodness, Beauty, Liberty, Equality, Justice* (the subject of a PBS series). Adler is perhaps most famous for his central role in selecting and editing the 54-volume Great Books of the Western World and for tirelessly promoting Great Books course discussions in homes, schools, and libraries across the country.

In 1947 Hutchins and Adler established the Great Books Foundation to provide the means of a genuine liberal education for all adults. In 1962 the Foundation started the Junior Great Books program, and by 1970, 48,000 children were enrolled in 3,200 groups in public and private schools across the country. In 1995, the National Endowment for the Humanities awarded the Great Books Foundation a grant based on the premise that Shared Inquiry was a powerful model for civil discourse in a democratic society. Shared Inquiry came into existence long before *The Paideia Proposal* was written, and The Great Books Foundation continues to put into practice much of Adler's liberal arts philosophy of education.

In 1979 Adler formed the Paideia Group, a committee of scholars including Jacques Barzun, Clifton Fadiman, Charles Van Doren, and Theodore Sizer, in order to bring the principles of liberal learning, as developed at the University of Chicago by Hutchins and Adler, to the primary and secondary school level. Their goal was not only to develop a better theory of education, but to form an organization to develop curricula, train teachers, and implement their ideas in actual classrooms. Instead of creating new schools, Paideia would bring classicism into existing school structures. Besides developing a liberal arts curriculum, Paideia also would establish a liberal arts pedagogy.

In 1982, on behalf of the members of the Paideia Group, Mortimer Adler wrote *The Paideia Proposal*, a four-part educational manifesto was the first of the Paideia Group's trilogy: *The Paideia Proposal, An Educational Manifesto* (1982), *Paideia Problems and Possibilities: A Consideration of Questions Raised by The Paideia Proposal* (1983), and *The Paideia Program* (1984). The publication of these books created much public interest across the country and, in response to many requests for training, Adler raised money and brought in principals nominated from around the states for a three-day retreat that focused on the Paideia project and implementation

In 1985 Adler formed the Paideia Associates, a group of sixteen individuals who demonstrated skill, knowledge, and interest in school reform. The Paideia Associates designed and conducted the early training and implementation programs and formulated "The Paideia Principles," a summary of the major points of the Paideia concept of education. These 12 principles were later published in *Reforming Education: The Opening of The American Mind*. By 1988, Adler's work led to the creation of the National Paideia Center and Paideia, Inc.

The Paideia Theory

Four years after the Paideia trilogy was complete, Paideia Group member Geraldine Van Doren collected 24 of Adler's essays in *Reforming Education: The Opening of the American Mind*. In one of the essays, Adler lays out his fundamental principles of education and asserts that "human nature is everywhere the same"; that man's capacities are not fully developed at birth; and that education is "the process whereby a man helps himself or another to become what he can be ... the process whereby a man is changed for the better." Education has a twofold end: the development of man's moral and intellectual virtues, and happiness, or the "life enriched by the possession of every kind of good" to which these virtues lead.[6]

Adler's theory follows the neoclassicism of the American founders and grounds the Paideia theory firmly on the premises of self-government, social equality, and individual freedom. This may be Adler's signal contribution in the modern revival of the tradition of classical education.

The first chapter of *The Paideia Proposal*, entitled "Democracy and Education," makes the connection clear: "Universal suffrage and universal schooling are inextricably bound together." Adler was inspired by John Dewey's 1916 *Democracy and Education*, going on to say that the revolutionary message of Dewey's book "was that a democratic society must provide equal opportunity not only by giving to all its children the same quantity of public education—the same number of years in school—but also by making sure to give to all of them, all with no exceptions, the same quality of education."[7]

Adler maintains that social equality requires the same quality of schooling for all. Committed to democracy, Adler opposes attempts to establish multiple education tracks for students of differing abilities and insists on a single-track system that gives every student the same educational opportunities.

Education is essential in a democracy because if citizens are to govern themselves wisely they must be able to make informed judgments about policies, understand the complexities of public issues, and be able to contribute to the deliberations of the republic. They also must have the intellectual sophistication to avoid a mob mentality and manipulation by demagogues who have been the wreck of earlier democracies. Adler cautions, "You may be apathetic about improving your own life. You may be relatively hopeless about seeing the promises of democracy reach their full fruition. But you cannot love your children and at the same time be callous about the betterment of their lives, together with the betterment of the society in which they will live as adults ... you cannot love your country and at the same time be indifferent about the future of its free institutions."[8]

The Practice

A truly democratic education gives all students the same liberal and general program of study and rejects all distractions. "All side-tracks, specialized courses, or elective choices must be eliminated." A smorgasbord of options makes education haphazard and incoherent, and it deprives students of the benefits of a cumulative educational curriculum.

The Paideia principles argue that "the three types of teaching that should occur in our schools are didactic teaching of subject matter, coaching that produces the skills of learning, and Socratic questioning in seminar discussion;" and "that the results of these three types of teaching should be (a) acquisition of organized knowledge, (b) the formation of habits of skill in the use of language and mathematics, and (c) the growth of the mind's understanding of basic ideas and issues"[9]

The three modes of teaching—didactic instruction, coaching, and Socratic questioning—correspond to the three ways the mind can be improved. The mind can be improved by the acquisition of knowledge, by the development of intellectual skills, and by the enlargement of understanding of ideas and values.

What kind of knowledge must be acquired? "There are three areas of subject matter indispensable to basic schooling: (1) language, literature, fine arts; (2) mathematics, natural sciences; (3) history, geography, and social studies." "No one," Adler insists, "can claim to be educated who is not reasonably well acquainted with all three."[10]

For Paideia educators, the three types of teaching—didactic instruction, intellectual coaching, and Socratic questioning—correspond to the three types of learning: acquiring knowledge, gaining skills, and enlarging understanding. Dr. Terry Roberts and Dr. Laura Billings of the National Paideia Center explain, "it is important to note that the Three Columns are best practiced in active synergy, such that each of the three modes of teaching reinforces the other two." A fully realized Paideia classroom "features units of study integrated across subject areas," and the Paideia teacher uses all three columns in a complementary manner when teaching.[11]

Higher-order thinking depends on a prior acquisition of knowledge and skills. But neither didactic instruction nor intellectual coaching is enough to fully understand and express ideas and principles. Enlarged understanding, Paideia's Column Three, arises from questioning and intellectual interaction. Adler claims that direct contact with works of art makes this possible. Literature, music, dance, drama, and painting engage the student's mind in a comprehensive way. They generate responses that compel students to agree or disagree, to defend an opinion, and ultimately to go beyond superficial emotional reactions.

To enlarge understanding, the teacher must employ the appropriate mode of instruction, which Adler calls "the Socratic mode of teaching, a mode of teaching called 'maieutic' [from the Greek word that means, "related to midwifery"] because it helps the student bring ideas to birth. It is teaching by asking questions, by leading discussions, by helping students to raise their minds up from a state of understanding or appreciating less to a state of understanding or appreciating more." Socratic teaching enlarges the understanding of the student by stimulating the imagination and intellect by awakening the creative and inquisitive powers. Adler says that "in no other way can children's understanding of what they know be improved, and their appreciation of cultural objects be enhanced."[12] The Socratic discussion centers around a text, a book, or product of human artistry.

Socratic discussions help to fulfill the objective of preparing young people to become intelligent citizens who have the knowledge and critical thinking skills necessary for reasoned discourse and well-mannered debate. "For mutual understanding and responsible debate among the citizens of a democratic community, and for differences of opinion to be aired and resolved, citizens must be able to communicate with one another in a common language."[13] The common language every citizen should know and speak is a vocabulary of ideas and principles discovered in a text through the art of Socratic conversation.

"The role of the Socratic teacher in a seminar is that of a good conversationalist who primes the pump of discussion by asking leading questions and pursuing the answers given to them by asking more questions."[14] Although there are different kinds of seminars for different kinds of books and different levels of students, the goals of the seminar are the same, namely "to bring out and then clarify the ideas and issues that are raised by something that has been read or otherwise experienced jointly by the leader and the students. A secondary goal of such teaching is to make clear the book or work of art itself."[15]

In the early 1940s the first type of Socratic seminar started to take shape in "Shared Inquiry." Today, at the Great Books Foundation, "Shared Inquiry" is a discussion method, a teaching and learning environment, and a way for individuals to achieve a more thorough understanding of a text by discussing questions, responses, and insights with fellow readers. For over 60 years the Great Books Foundation has shown that engaging students in well-managed conversations helps students develop higher-order thinking and problem-solving skills. "In Shared Inquiry, participants come together to help each other explore the meaning of a work of literature. Each participant brings a unique perspective that influences how he or she understands the work. Sharing their interpretations, participants gain new insights and deepen or even change their initial understanding." The goal of Shared Inquiry is to "instill in adults and children the habits of mind that characterize self-reliant thinkers, readers, and learners." Like Adler, Shared Inquiry assumes that "everyone can read and understand excellent literature—literature that has the capacity to engage the whole person, the imagination as well as the intellect." Although the Great Books Foundation does not promote itself as Paideia, Shared Inquiry is democratic classicism; it "promotes thoughtful dialogue and open debate, preparing its participants to become able, responsible citizens, and enthusiastic, life-long readers."[16]

The National Paideia Center defines its Paideia Seminar as a collaborative, intellectual dialogue facilitated with open-ended questions about a text.[17] Paideia Seminars are designed to improve the individual's ability to explain and manipulate complex systems. The specific learning objectives for Paideia Seminar include both intellectual and social skills. The National Paideia Center does not teach the generic "Socratic Seminar"; instead

NPC Paideia Seminar leaders ask very deliberately formed questions. The opening questions in an NPC Paideia Seminar are "maieutic," the core questions are "Socratic," and the closing questions are "maieutic."

Roberts and Billings wrote *Teaching Critical Thinking, Using Seminars for 21st Century Literacy* with the goal of helping teachers prepare their students to lead richer, more thoughtful lives in at least three ways: "by being good citizens when democratic citizenship—whether local or global— requires objectivity and understanding, by leading good lives, honoring our own hearts, minds, and souls as well as those of others, [and] by earning decent livings in what many commentators are calling the 'Cognitive Age.'"[18] The way the Paideia Seminars teach the skills of critical thinking amounts to "classical education intended for the 21st century. It involves returning to ancient wisdom as a response to contemporary challenges."[19]

The National Paideia Center offers professional development to teachers and principals through events, materials, memberships, and whole-school implementation plans. Offering institutes and an annual international Paideia conference, the National Paideia Center teaches educators the skills and strategies to help them engage students in actual learning, lead students and faculty in intellectual and collaborative dialogue, and improve student achievement. Additionally, the NPC offers model seminar lesson plans designed to enhance the delivery of teachers' curriculum.

By 2012, the National Paideia Center had several schools in the whole-school Paideia Program implementation process, with many more developing parts of the Paideia program. Since its founding in 1988, the National Paideia Center has worked with hundreds of schools in the United States and the District of Columbia, as well as one school in the Philippines.

Paideia Group, Inc. offers professional development to educators through on-site teacher training, select reading materials, starter sets for sample units, a national conference for teachers and principals, news-letters, and certification programs for Paideia teachers. Committed to the Paideia Group's vision embodied in the Paideia trilogy, for nearly 30 years, Dr. Patricia Weiss has been cultivating Paideia principles in schools across America.

Dr. Patricia Weiss and Dr. Anne Kaufman, director of the Augsburg Paideia Group, have been working together for nearly 25 years. Since 1988, the Augsburg Paideia Group has hosted an annual Augsburg Paideia Institute. The Augsburg Paideia Institute is open not only to public school teachers, but to any and all who want to learn how to implement Paideia principles in the classroom. The key elements in the Augsburg Paideia Institute are didactic teaching for the retention of facts and information, coaching for skill development, and Socratic seminars for enhanced under-standing of ideas. In this five-day institute, Augsburg offers experience and practice in seminars, debriefings, small group sessions, coaching, curriculum development, and writing. Most of Kaufman's recent work has been done with charter schools, and one in particular, St. Croix Preparatory Academy in Stillwater, Minnesota. Kaufman and Weiss trained over 60 teachers from St. Croix in 2010–12, and St. Croix Preparatory Academy has incorporated Paideia seminars at all grade levels and in all subject areas. Besides St. Croix, since 2003 the Augsburg Paideia Institute has trained nearly 100 - charter schools.

The Great Books Foundation also offers professional development through core sequence courses, on-site consultation, and curriculum resources. For seven decades the work of the Great Books Foundation has continued to build upon Hutchins and Adler's insistence on timeless literature and the benefits of discussion. Today the Foundation's resources include a plethora of classroom products for all grade levels, Junior Great Books lists, new publications, recommended readings for book groups and colleges, discussion guides for selected books, and the Great Books online bookstore.

Research shows that seminars can be used to improve standardized test scores: end-of-grade tests improved in reading and mathematics after one year of seminar implementation, and top students continued to increase their scores. Paideia students had a higher average daily attendance, and even resulted in a reduction in the achievement gap between African-American and Caucasian students. In addition, research shows that both teachers and principals value Paideia Seminars. One principal observed that the seminars teach students "how to engage in civil dialogue, think critically, and look at both sides of issues. Because students learn how to agree to disagree, a Paideia school environment is really positive."[20]

As we look at the research results of schools that have attempted to give themselves in part or whole to Paideia Principles, it is important to recall what Adler taught about the serious mistake we make in measuring Paideia. The mistake "consists in thinking that equality of opportunity can be expected to lead to equality of results."[21] Adler adds, "the very opposite is to be expected. The equality of all the children as human beings, an equality that derives from their common humanity and personhood, is accompanied by individual inequality in talents and aptitudes."[22] Ultimate outcomes will differ between students because of individual inequality. In short, no standardized test can measure Paideia's success because humans are persons, and persons are individuals. In truth, many of the benefits of intellectual coaching and Socratic discussion can never be captured in a formal review.

In the introduction to *The Paideia Program*, Adler emphasized that the primary objective of *The Paideia Proposal* was to democracy and to a democratic system of public schooling. The mandate was to provide equal education to all, not by giving children only the same quantity of schooling, but also the same quality of schooling. Adler hoped to build a truly democratic school system by the end of the twentieth century "in order that our democratic institution may be strengthened, in order that our economy may prosper, and in order that our future citizens may be able to enjoy the quality of life that should be vouchsafed every human being."[23]

However, in reality there are very few true Paideia schools, schools that realize the ideas set forth in *The Paideia Proposal* and the practices suggested in *The Paideia Program*. But the National Paideia Center, Paideia Group, Inc., Augsburg Paideia Group, and individual charter schools across the country are still striving to implement parts of the Paideia vision, with many different public and charter schools in many different phases of development. In short, Paideia is still being implemented in part, but not in whole. Because of the efforts of educational reformers like Dr. Terry Roberts, Dr. Laura Billings, Dr. Patricia Weiss, and Dr. Anne Kaufman, the vision of Robert Hutchins, Mortimer Adler, and the Paideia Group has not been lost. Paideia, the hope of democratic classicism and the dream of equal educational opportunity, still lives.

Great Hearts Academies

It lives, for example, in Phoenix, Arizona, where democratic classicism was firmly planted in 2002 with the founding of Veritas Preparatory Academy, the first of a dozen Great Hearts schools scattered throughout the Phoenix metropolitan area. Great Hearts Academies is a charter school initiative that has proved a resounding success, serving over 6,000 students on twelve campuses, with active plans for expansion into San Antonio, Texas, and Nashville, Tennessee.

As a charter school umbrella, Great Hearts is designed to provide an alternative to a "large, inefficient [Phoenix public school system which] does not enforce clear goals for student formation and achievement." Central to this effort to reclaim public education is the notion of "formation," since it is their expressed desire to train leaders "of character who will contribute to a more philosophical, humane, and just society." Such language permeates Great Hearts literature along with frequent invoking of the classical virtues of "the good, the true, and the beautiful," and to the liberal arts as the foundation of "each student's quest to live as a free citizen of the West."[24]

To be free, one must have the critical-thinking skills that inoculate against the alluring rhetoric that pervades contemporary society, rhetoric that is constantly seeking to undermine freedom for the sake of varied narrow interests. It is an old story, and Daniel Scoggin, the CEO of Great Hearts, recognizes this reality when he reminds his constituency that "each generation must earn its freedom anew."[25]

This kind of language clearly evokes the ideas of Mortimer Adler and his Paideia movement. Yet one is hard-pressed to find explicit references to Adler or to Paideia in Great Hearts materials (though in job descriptions Adler's name does seem to be prominent, and individual schools' websites do invoke his name). Nevertheless, their debt to Adler's ideas about education is clear upon even a cursory reading of their philosophical pillars and school model. First and foremost, Great Hearts Academies are public classical schools. In addition, like Adler, Great Hearts believes that "good habits of virtue cannot simply be taught, but must be modeled, reflected upon, and experienced through immersion" (emphasis added). Reflecting Adler's commitment to democracy, Great Hearts "offers the same academically rigorous program to all students and has no admissions criteria." This extends even to the provision of special education services, something which many private classical schools are unable to do. Also reflecting Adler's belief that the best education is education for all, Great Hearts offers a one-track educational model that includes "no electives," with the exception—again like Adler—of modern foreign languages in the high school years.

We noted earlier that Adler eschewed use of the term "classical" to describe his approach to education. Great Hearts Academies, unlike Adler on this point, prominently proclaim their commitment to classical education as such, as is seen in its school motto: "Classical Education, Revolutionary Schools." References to Dorothy Sayers are not difficult to find, particularly in their annual journal Great Hearts, and they are not averse to claiming to have incorporated those "lost tools of learning" into their own pedagogical edifice, albeit much more in the manner of Adler than in the manner of, for example, the Association of Classical Christian Schools. In terms of the debate over what constitutes "classical"—and especially whether to emphasize Greece and Rome (what we may call "classical proper") or to engage "classics" in the sense of anything of enduring value produced in the West—Great Hearts Academies follow Adler and subscribe to the latter view.

Great Hearts began their mission with the founding of upper schools, grades 6-12, and after the founding of Veritas Prep in 2002, there followed, among others, Chandler Prep (2004), Mesa Prep (2006), Glendale and Scottsdale Preps (2007), down to North Phoenix Prep, founded in 2011 with 176 students on opening day.

What we have written so far reflects primarily a focus on upper-level schooling, but, with the upper-school model well-developed and demand for a Great Hearts education resoundingly demonstrated, attention turned to developing the "classical elementary school." Not surprisingly, this enlargement of vision soon developed: the first of these Great Hearts "Archway" schools (grades K–5), Archway Chandler, was founded in 2009. Now a half-dozen Archways boast a combined enrollment of some 2,400 students.

The Archway schools do make use of some standardized curricula; for example, the use of Singapore Math and of Core Knowledge for history, science, music, and art. Nevertheless, the upper-school commitment to the primary text is evident even in this grammar school setting, with an extensive list of great books appropriate for grades K–5. Notable also in their curriculum is the pace of mathematical instruction. The math preparation at the "Archway" level allows students to begin pre-Algebra in the sixth grade, followed by a more-or-less standard sequence of math that, because of its acceleration, allows for a two-year encounter with the "beauty of the calculus" in the junior and senior years.

The practice of teaching in the Great Hearts Academies mirrors Adler's three-column approach, without naming it. The elementary years are focused on knowledge acquisition, but not without an admixture of both coaching and the Socratic method. As students graduate to higher levels of achievement, the mixture changes to focus on coaching and then, in the high school years, to focus on a "Socratic engagement of students" over the primary texts that form the basis for their discussions. In the humanities in the upper school years (grades 6-12), only primary sources—i.e., the great books themselves—are used; secondary sources are ignored, enabling the students to engage great literature on its own terms, rather than through the lens of a textbook writer who will fade into obscurity while the great work's author will endure. Great Hearts schools approach their texts from an explicitly "new critical" point of view. The New Criticism is a mid-twentieth-century school of thought that largely grew out of Vanderbilt University and the writings of John Crowe Ransom and Robert Penn Warren, among others, and so was somewhat identified with "Southern Agrarianism." It emphasized the aesthetics of the text to be studied, understanding the text to be an object unto itself that carried meaning apart from historical context, authorial intent, or the response of the reader. This emphasis on aesthetics well agrees with the overall goals of the Great Hearts commitment to *verum, pulchrum, bonum* "the true, the beautiful, and the good."

Hillsdale Academy

Whereas Great Hearts Academies began as upper schools that grew into the lower grades, Hillsdale Academy was founded in 1990 as a K–8 extension of Hillsdale College, ultimately growing into the upper grades, and now constituting a school that, other than being private, in many ways mirrors the pedagogical thought of Mortimer Adler.

Hillsdale Academy was begun by Hillsdale College to extend the College's mission into secondary education in order "to teach students to love virtue and wisdom and to develop the habits of self-government."[26] The need for an excellent education was particularly acute given the College's geographic location in one of the poorest counties in Michigan, with correspondingly poor opportunities for public education. In the years that data is available (1998—the founding the upper school—to the present), Hillsdale Academy has seen a general trend of growth, drawing students from three counties, and serves 200 students in grades K–12.[27]

Hillsdale Academy's mission is, like the College's, to deliver an education both liberal and civic, that is, to educate students in the classical liberal arts while also developing civic virtue informed by the Western tradition in its Judaeo-Christian and Greco-Roman roots. The founding principles of the United States, as expressed in the Constitution and Declaration of Independence, are primary in the theory and practice of a Hillsdale Academy education. Many schools that participate in the classical education renaissance are founded on explicitly Christian—and even particularly denominational—lines, but although a Hillsdale education is informed by theological and biblical principles that arise from the Western tradition, religion as such does not form an integral part of the curriculum or the daily culture of the school. Nevertheless, fundamental to the Hillsdale education is the belief that truth exists and that it can be known through the exercise of reason, and that there are objective standards of beauty and virtue.

Hillsdale Academy's principled commitment to its educational model—a reflection of its parent institution—has not led it into isolation from the wider educational community. For example, on the one hand, Hillsdale Academy has chosen not to pursue accreditation—even private accreditation, because accreditation would make them beholden to modern pedagogical ideas they find inimical to their own model (including increased use of technology for its own sake, requirements for "sex education," and teacher certification that "overthrows the authority of the teacher"). Kenneth Calvert, headmaster of Hillsdale Academy, observes that accreditation "has come to mean little or nothing."[28] On the other hand, although Hillsdale does not "teach to the test," it does participate in standardized testing. Students' performance on the Iowa Test of Basic Skills and the high school Advanced Placement exams (the latter taken "cold") at once serves as a measure against other schools and indicates on some level the effectiveness of their model.[29] Given the School's relatively small student body, Hillsdale has had a disproportionately large number of National Merit Scholars, and their students score well on other standardized tests.

One particular area in which Hillsdale Academy departs from the Adlerian view of education is its attitude toward the work of John Dewey. Whereas Adler and his associates believed Dewey was a "great American educator," Hillsdale's education explicitly rejects Dewey's call for educators to move away from classroom rigor into creativity and self-expression. Likewise, Hillsdale sees Dewey's sensory, group-oriented approach as inimical to the education of a free individual.[30] Instead, Hillsdale expressly seeks to return to the ancients "who teach a wisdom of human experience." Hillsdale believes that the person can be improved through *habit* but no community will ever become that utopia (contrary to many "Progressives" in our own day). The utopianism of the Progressives of the last century and a half has ultimately led to bloodshed on a scale never before imagined. But with Aristotle, Hillsdale seeks to inculcate a habit of seeking the good, which is essential to happiness and to the flourishing of human communities.

Hillsdale College and Hillsdale Academy recently created a Liberal Arts Teaching Apprenticeship. Twenty applicants are accepted into the program each year, and each apprentice spends time teaching, observing, preparing tests, etc., in the classrooms at Hillsdale Academy. The program was created when Hillsdale discovered that, out of their graduates who were employed teaching, 50 percent were teaching in non-public schools, and half of those had not completed an education program. Thus, the program prepares apprentices to teach and administer schools in the Hillsdale classical liberal arts tradition.

The Barney Charter Initiative

Taking advantage of the Teaching Apprenticeship are schools in the newly formed Barney Charter Initiative, sponsored by Hillsdale College and a sister effort to Hillsdale Academy. Adlerian classicism is a pedagogical school of thought aimed at government-run education. Hillsdale Academy, for all its similarity to Adler, is private. But in 2009, the Barney Family Foundation provided the seed money for the "Barney Charter Initiative," an effort also sponsored by Hillsdale College that is intended to bring Hillsdale's particular brand of democratic classicism to a public school setting.

The Barney Charter Initiative was created to address the pressing question, "How can we lead in the effort to recover our government-run schools from the tide of one hundred years of progressivism that has corrupted our nation's original faithfulness to the previous twenty-four centuries of teaching the young the liberal arts in the West?" Hillsdale College has diagnosed the same public school malady that Great Hearts Academies has diagnosed, but is pursuing its prescription in a somewhat different way. Whereas Great Hearts has grown organically within its native Phoenix area and only later looked to expand into other metropolitan areas, the Barney Initiative was conceived as "national" in scope from the outset; national in the sense that any sufficiently organized body in any locality may seek its sponsorship. For example, in Lewisville, Texas, an existing charter school organization joined forces with the Barney Charter School Initiative to open Founders Classical Academy. In contrast, Estancia Valley Classical Academy in Moriarty, New Mexico, was founded by a "was founded by a group of concerned community members who aim to counter the trend of academic mediocrity and cultural illiteracy in America"[31]

The Barney Initiative is still young: Founders Classical Academy and

Estancia Valley Classical Academy both began operations in August 2012. Two more schools, in Savannah, Georgia, and Bentonville, Arkansas, opened in 2013, while 2014 saw four more (in Atlanta; Las Vegas; Naples, Florida; and Leander, Texas). In 2015, another two schools will open in Golden, Colorado, and Palm Bay, Florida.[32] Still more groups from around the United States seek the sponsorship of the Barney Charter School Initiative. If the remarkable growth of Great Hearts schools is any indication of the future of Barney Initiative Schools, then democratic classicism in public schools across the United States will continue to grow and exert an ever wider and more profound influence.

V

Norms and Nobility

In the United States many private schools have offered classical education for generations. Even the phrase "Latin school" occasionally appears in their names. Despite our long-standing tradition of public education, leaders in business, politics, and the professions have been nourished by America's network of private academies, whose reputation for excellence attracts families who can afford the best for their children. Indeed, any number of prominent politicians who vehemently defend government-run schools send their own children to private academies.

As a rule, these private academies continue to provide a higher quality of education than most government schools, but some believe they have lost their way. Writing in *Inform* magazine, Richard Hawley points out that, "The founding purpose of America's great schools was the production of virtue." Everything changed in the 1960s, as it did in the wider culture. "Aware for perhaps the first time in private school history that their traditional customers were finding prep schools resistible, the schools began testing the market." A great change occurred: Private schools began to treat education as a marketplace commodity, and they accommodated the demands of their customers instead of holding parents to a higher ideal.

Schools tested the market and discovered that children preferred to avoid hard work and rules on clothing, grooming, and free time. Children especially disliked schools that enrolled only one sex. Parents made other demands that were "not only demonstrably bad for children but self-contradictory." Parents demanded high academic standards but wanted no challenges that might undermine a child's self-esteem; they accepted inflated grades but expected schools to expunge records that took notice of failure.

By trying to accommodate consumer demands, the great private schools disarmed themselves in the cultural battles of the 1960s. When young people cloaked their craving for adolescent freedom with the aura of justice and proclaimed a new spiritual and ethical vision, the schools were morally exhausted and found their demands impossible to resist. They gave their customers what they demanded.

Not only did the collapse of standards permanently alter the face of America but, according to Hawley, it endangered the very existence of traditional private schools. The market to which they have catered is doing what markets often do—letting customers drive the offerings. Hawley observes that, "in their worries over their declining market appeal, even the most long-standing and substantial American boarding schools have, over the past quarter century, given up their reason for being."

David Hicks has been a teacher and headmaster at a number of these academies, and he has given much thought to the nature of classical education. Hawley's *Inform* article was a response to one by Hicks in the American Scholar entitled, "The Strange Fate of the American Boarding School." Hicks had asserted that, "Like the American family itself, these schools have been largely deconstructed and are in danger of becoming dysfunctional."

Hicks agreed that modern American culture was greatly responsible for dismantling private academies, but he argued that educational theory is also to blame.

"Contributing to the deconstruction of these schools is the fragmenting effect of descriptive developmental theories that have replaced the prescriptive moral aims of an earlier time .... The student's self-esteem is all important, and it is better to affirm the adolescent in the quest [for identity apart from standards] than to hold him or her accountable to some prescriptive norm or arbitrary standard and thereby constrain self-expression and wound self-esteem." When children need wise, normative guidance, they are sent alone on a journey the purpose and nature of which they cannot understand.

In his book *Norms and Nobility: A Treatise on Education* (1981), Hicks develops these ideas into a comprehensive theory of education. He places special emphasis on the importance of teaching morality and fostering virtue that characterizes the classical approach to learning but noticeable by its absence in most contemporary schools. *Norms and Nobility* offers a modern curriculum and methodology based on classical standards and ideals that have guided Hicks' work as headmaster of several leading American independent schools, a conference speaker, and a consultant.

If the ACCS offers a Christian classicism and Paideia champions a democratic classicism, Hicks can be described as a spokesman for what he calls a "normative classicism." Each approach to classicism described here rests on somewhat different philosophical foundations, though their intentions and methods are quite similar and compatible. Douglas Wilson is an Augustinian: his school teaches with systematic rigor, but it does so with an awareness of human sin, the need for God's grace, and God's sovereignty over all of life, positions that characterize Wilson's specifically Reformed, Calvinist theology (a species of Augustinianism). Mortimer Adler was an Aristotelian, and the Paideia proposal reflects the scrutiny of purpose, making of distinctions, and commonsense rationalism that are Aristotle's legacy to Western thought. Hicks finds inspiration in the ideals of Plato. He builds his educational theory on a search for the ideal and a conviction that education should be a path to virtue. His curriculum is akin to the classical humanism of the Renaissance, which studies the humanistic disciplines to cultivate man's potential.

For Hicks, "The mastery of thinking skills and the understanding of basic ideas in our Western (or any other) intellectual tradition" are insufficient ends for education. Instead, he argues from his experiences that if a school's goals are limited to producing students who are rational thinkers, they will fail even at that. "Education," Hicks insists, "must address the whole student, his emotional and spiritual sides as well as his rational."[1]

Hicks understands that his call for a normative and prescriptive education is controversial. But he believes it is justified by its honesty. All education is normative. The difference for the classical educator is that he makes known the norms that guide him. "The aims of education, the teacher's methods, the books and lessons, the traditions, and the regulations of the school—all must express not just ideas, but norms, tending to make young people not only rational, but noble." This is fitting, since students cannot discover their own norms in isolation, as evidenced by the acknowledged need for coaches, mentors, and music teachers, not to mention parents.

A Christian, Hicks describes his vision of a genuinely Christian paideia. One of his governing ideas is the necessity of dogma. But he adds that, in practice, dogma is the springboard, not the pool. Dogma makes serious inquiry possible; it does not end it. Hicks believes that we see through a glass darkly in the City of Man, this side of Plato's realm of ideal forms—we gain only provisional answers approximating truth, to be tested by reason and to be constantly applied and refined in the life of the student. Hicks' curriculum contains Christian and non-Christian books and ideas, all investigated normatively and Socratically, exploring their ideas and their relations to each other. "In classical education, the connection between dogma and dialectic defines the master-pupil relationship."[2]

But Hicks has strong words for the feigned neutrality of the analytical educator. Because he insists on teaching the whole child in all his domains, Hicks asserts that the exclusion of dogma not only prevents the child from engaging one of his essential elements, it also leads the teacher into the self-delusion—or outward deception—of neutrality.

Abandoning a self-consciously normative education, the modern school "adopts a posture of non-dogmatic, value-free learning that is not only false, but dangerous." Dangerous, because this posture can only be a deception, for modern educators also need and make use of dogma. They disguise their dogma through distraction: "by subjecting all content to doubt, while granting analytical form the status of an incontrovertible dogma."[3]

And indeed, since Hicks wrote *Norms and Nobility* in 1981, education has become increasingly ideological, holding to unacknowledged dogma and thereby removing its own dogma from the challenges of dialectical engagement. "Teachers are discouraged from teaching themselves, and students are asked to judge ideas in analytical detachment on the basis of unverifiable ideological presuppositions."[4]

The Theory

Education, argues Hicks, used to be very different from the conventional activities practiced in its name. The present clash is between the normative and the analytical. In the ancient world, teachers and students learned together in an atmosphere dominated by what Hicks calls the Ideal Type. The Ideal Type is an image of the fully developed human being.

Because educators accepted the Ideal as a model or prototype, their instruction was aimed at cultivating within individuals what we now call "the whole person." The educational Ideal informed what the individual aspired to become; it expressed what religion taught as God's will for mankind; and it incorporated the most elevated components of what classical culture held up for admiration.

The rise of "modern" philosophy changed all that. The Ideal Type was replaced by scientific method, which reduced the reality of the Ideal to the particularity of atomized individuals whose traits could be measured. Descartes, according to Hicks, led the philosophical attack on the spirit of classical education by arguing "that education ought to concern itself only with ideas that are precise and certain beyond any possibility of doubt."

This redefinition of man's humanity (what C. S. Lewis called "the Abolition of Man"[5]) excluded the rich complexities of the spirit—will, conscience, and moral character—from the realm of education. The most important dimensions of human life were no longer considered valid subjects for "the great conversation" of the liberal arts curriculum unless they could be made consistent with the new "scientific method." Religion, history, and literature courses were no longer expected to tell the truth about man's nature and purposes. At best, they commented on the misconceptions of those who had not yet attained the certainties of the quantitative sciences.

A new educational and philosophical language developed to reflect the new scientific theory. It was the non-normative language of materialism, utilitarianism, and pragmatism. With it, one discussed the tangible, the finite, and the material. The new methods, which Hicks summarizes under the term "analytical," agreed that the intangible, infinite, and immaterial were literally inconceivable.

Because modern education theory draws heavily on the legacy of modern scientific philosophy, Hicks observes that it ignores anything that cannot be precisely measured. By definition, the infinite is beyond measurement, as are ethical truths, creativity, and human worth. Contemporary proponents of the modern school boldly promise to save society if only their ways are adopted, thus importing their dogma. But Hicks answers that education policies built solely around attempts to measure and quantify learning—from standardized tests to government policies like Race to the Top and Common Core—will continue to fail because they exclude the intangible qualities of personality and character that make up the human spirit.

The goal of the modern school, says Hicks, is to prepare students for a materially efficient existence—for the achievement of selfish and tangible personal ends. This kind of education also serves the needs of the state and the economy. To promote these goals, students are taught facts: knowledge that is precise, certain, and limited. They are also taught programs—or rather, they are programmed—in repetitive and highly functional techniques to perform roles necessary for the smooth running of society.

Society, however, is in a state of moral collapse because, Hicks argues, it has rejected the infinite and the intangible. Crime, drug abuse, divorce, and other social pathologies are the measurable proof of the anxieties of the moral vacuum in which modern youth live. "Trapped by the logic of their positivist presuppositions, both school and society grasp at material straws in the winds of spiritual dissolution and decay."[6] In short, Hicks believes we suffer from a blurred vision of education that no longer sees the personal value of knowledge in a life of virtue.

From the ancient world to the Renaissance, argues Hicks, the goal of learning was not merely to amass information or attain job skills, but above all to cultivate virtue. Classical education showed individuals the Ideal Type representing what they should be. The Ideal Type was more than a sentimental aspiration: it could be achieved by intellect, effort, and habit. To the ancients, a life of virtue was synonymous with the full development of a person's essential humanity. The cultivation and growth of our best nature was considered the true and final goal of education. Classical education, defined by Hicks as "a spirit of inquiry and a form of instruction concerned with the development of style through language and of conscience through myth," was the best way to achieve this goal.

The Practice

Hicks believes the normative concept of the "Ideal Type" should shape the content of education and the modes of teaching. Teachers should not merely help students become successful in their careers. They should ask, "How can I cultivate virtue within them?"

For instance, classical schools should be selective about what students read. Such schools will prefer time-honored books to those that super-ficially reflect current trends. History will be studied without cynicism, and ancient soul-nourishing myths, folk tales, and Bible stories will be cherished. Even science will be taught in the light of virtue. The classical science teacher, says Hicks, constantly asks, "'How does scientific truth touch my students' lives and increase their understanding of themselves and their purposes?' A resolution of values must attend the study of science. Scientific analysis must be framed within normative inquiry if science is to serve life, not destroy it."

The first characteristic of a classical school, according to Hicks, is its reliance on dialectic. "Everything begins with the questions," says Hicks, and "the great thing about classical literature is that it forces you to ask the great questions … and that is what has always driven and informed classical education."[7]

Dialectic, too, is determined by a vision of virtue. The back and forth, give and take of questioning and discussion clarifies the role of the teacher, the use of language, and the right attitude toward knowledge. How does this process conduce to achieving virtue? Hicks explains that while analysis stands outside investigation and speaks with the voice of objectivity, dialectic is a more humane, intimate approach that engages the subject of investigation and speaks with the voice of involvement. It engages the particular issue from the perspective of the whole, and the whole from the particular. Mental processes that are reduced solely to analysis, on the other hand, exclude too many areas of inquiry. Dialectic permits and encourages rational discussions of virtue, goodness, beauty, and all the infinite and intangible things that escape analysis. All method in the classical school involves the application of dialectic.

In practice, the educational journey towards knowledge of truth does not begin with Descartes' skepticism; it begins with the sincere acceptance of dogma. *Dogma* is a Greek word meaning "that which seems good." It serves the vision of the whole by faithfully reproducing the true life of the mind, which is utterly incapable of beginning with doubt. Classical teachers must be dogmatic teachers in the sense that they cannot be skeptical or neutral toward knowledge. Instead, they must be committed and responsible to knowable truth.

And yet classical learning is neither doctrinaire religious instruction nor analytical scientific positivism. Like everybody else, though with an added touch of self-awareness, the classical student begins by accepting dogma, but he personalizes it by questioning—that is, by employing dialectic. As the student refines his understanding, his insight grows, "ascending a dialectical staircase to an upper room of fragile truths and intangible beliefs." Challenges and contradictions arise to and within dogma by the process of dialectic, and this leads to dogma's reformulation to better align with truth. Using his conscience and the process of dialectic, and guided by the universal vision of the Ideal Type, the student grows toward the ideal. Commitment to dogma and dialectic is thus the first principle in Hicks' version of classical education: the conscious development of the internal dialogue guides us to the fulfillment of our natures.

The second principle of classical education is what Hicks describes as "teaching the father of the man." It turns the modern Romantic "child-centered" approach to education right side up. Latter-day Romantic educators have a naïve understanding of a child's nature and misapprehend what it takes to teach children. Hicks remarks, "Developmental theories stress the adolescent's search for identity and the importance of freedom and experimentation in making the quest, and with these theories comes an overwhelming emphasis on the individual, even at the expense of the community, and on personality as defined by one's inner feelings and appetites rather than on character as formed by codes of conduct and standards of behavior that exist outside and prior to the individual." They believe childhood is a time set aside for pleasure and freedom because they want learning to be fun and entertaining, scarcely distinguishable from games and play.

The classical teacher sees childhood very differently. He knows that "children ... want to be brought up; they do not want to remain 12-year-olds." The teacher aims to form the adult-to-be, not to liberate the child within. He also realizes, with Aristotle, that "All men by nature desire to know."

Thus, the classical teacher's curriculum is knowledge-centered and inquiry-based. It is ordered toward knowing truths. The modern teacher considers this type of learning too difficult and of little relevance to the child's experience. But the goal of the classical teacher is to feed the child life-nourishing matter, truths, and virtues that help the child grow into adulthood. The challenge of classical teaching, according to Hicks, is "to understand what form advanced concepts ought to take at a rudimentary level of psychological development, while it is the challenge of learning to discipline the unruly and discursive mind, adjusting its disorderliness through rigorous study to the order of logical processes found outside it in the subject matter."

Classical teachers make their students work hard. In fact, some will assign the hardest studies first because they believe that a student who can master these will handle all that follows. Says Hicks: "Put thus abstractly and unconditionally, the classical approach sounds harsh indeed—and I would be inclined to doubt its efficacy were it not for the piano lessons of my boyhood days." Hicks describes the lessons he learned when a lax and too-obliging teacher had him play a one-note "samba" from a book of graded exercises. Four years later he finished his graded exercises "with a banal rendition of something entitled 'the Lone Ranger.' By contrast, a friend who studied under a different tutor was expected to memorize and practice a simple minuet by Mozart and went on to play "with elegance and precision the Brahms, Chopin, and Liszt that my illiterate fingers will never coax out of a keyboard."

The classical approach teaches students difficult materials so they will develop their capacities toward an ideal. The process succeeds through the close relationship of teacher and pupil who work together in an atmosphere of love and responsibility. Students who approach subjects dialectically will develop skills of reason and analysis; they also will learn the moral responsibility that accompanies knowledge.

Centered on Humane Letters

The course of instruction that embodies this philosophy is described in the second half of *Norms and Nobility* in a section entitled, "The Practice of Classical Education." Hicks proposes three schools—maths and sciences, arts and languages, and humane letters—working in harmony to serve the normative goals of the academy: "to form the conscience and style of each student through the study of great art, basic science, and good letters."

Hicks argues that the humane letters, or humanities, should be at the center of the classical academy. Only the humanities have the power to integrate all elements of the curriculum, teach ethics and cultural norms, and help students develop social and communication skills by creating a school-based community that fosters the exchange of ideas.

Other classes should be coordinated around the humanities to complement its work. For instance, when students read the philosophy of ancient Greece, they also may learn to draw classical columns in their fine arts class. When they study the literature and politics of the Baroque era, they might rehearse Bach's *St. Matthew's Passion*.

Furthermore, the humanities teacher pays particular attention to the practice of dialogue. When students read great books they are encouraged to think of themselves as engaged in dialogue with the great authors of the world. The dialogue between student and text continues in class, where it is joined by the teacher and then by other students. A teacher in the school of humane letters engages the class in the study of literature, grammar, logic, history, philosophy, and religion. Students learn by reading classic texts that open avenues of insight into perennial questions; then, together, they enter into a dialogue begun in the ancient world. The teacher serves students both as a model and a co-participant who can help them develop an intellectual style and a moral conscience.

Reflecting in his preface to the second edition of *Norms and Nobility*, Hicks offers counsel on how to approach great works of literature. "Although in my curriculum proposal I use history as the paradigm for contextual learning, the ethical question 'What should one do?' might provide an even richer context for acquiring general knowledge. This question elicits not only knowledge, but wisdom, and it draws the interest of the student into any subject, no matter how obscure or far removed from his day-to-day concerns."[8] Many teachers and home school parents have confirmed Hicks' insight as they have worked with children using classical rhetoric programs like The Lost Tools of Writing,[9] which build the essay on "should" questions like "Should Brutus have killed Caesar?" or "Should Edmund have followed the White Witch?"

For Hicks, a classical school should offer a uniform and comprehensive curriculum, rather than an unfocused eclecticism and a proliferation of elective courses. Hicks argues that the intended purpose of electives—to allow students to pursue diverse interests—is actually implicit in a unified curriculum that urges the mind to recognize the intricacy of the whole and to thrive on making connections among its parts. "The beauty of the classical curriculum is that it dwells on one problem, one author, or one epoch long enough to allow even the youngest student a chance to exercise his mind in a scholarly way: to make connections and to trace developments, lines of reasoning, patterns of action, recurring symbolisms, plots, and motifs."

Integrating Math and Science

In a classical school, the school of mathematics and sciences is treated differently than in most contemporary schools. Math and science are neither abstract, self-sufficient learning goals nor tools for later job success. Instead, they are part of the classical curriculum's design to teach virtue and to enable the student to perceive truth.

Students do not learn the principles and reasoning of mathematics merely to find the correct answer. The classical approach disciplines the mind in concentration, memory, and logical process. Hicks argues that "the cumulative and coherent study of mathematics is, in fact, a microcosm of the entire curriculum and reflects in its expanding field the workings of the scholarly mind."

Likewise, the classical school teaches science in the context of human flourishing. We cannot know human beings as we know the material universe. "Contrary to their modern offspring," Hicks points out, "the ancients did not believe that man could learn about himself simply by asking the same analytical questions and by applying the same empirical methods as he might in his inquiry concerning the nature of the material universe." The classical school does not exclude science, but it subordinates it to the branches of learning that offer higher insights into human life. And in so doing, the teacher elevates the study of science by continually asking what our discoveries teach us about the human condition and our lives on earth.

The School of Arts and Languages trains students to discriminate as well as to participate in arts and languages. From the classical perspective, the arts have intrinsic value independent of social or political ends. They may be studied for vocational or recreational purposes, but their value is innate. Writes Hicks, "It is probably true that the study of art is no more essential than the civilization that it sustains."

Through the arts, students train their senses to perceive the world outside their minds. At the same time, they learn under the tutelage of the great artists to perceive realities they cannot easily see with their unaided and untrained eyes. Art integrates the ubiquitous appeal of self-expression with the material of other classes, rather than offering an isolated studio for a self-expression that students are ill-equipped to practice. Consequently, the classical student is better situated to make art than the student who, on the one hand, has been called to self-expression, but who, on the other hand, has been denied—because of the narrowness of his analytical curriculum— the opportunity to explore dimensions of his own being that would enrich the self he expresses.

Norms Do Not Oppress, They Raise Up

The old elite boarding schools in America and England may have been for the children of the wealthy and privileged, but it is remarkable how little they pampered their charges. Hicks notes that while their parents might live in great mansions, the children lived in Spartan conditions at school. School culture, with its uniforms and rituals, put everyone on an equal footing, and the student waited on by servants at home was expected to work hard at school. Wealthy parents sent their children to private schools so they would not grow up weak, lazy, or dissipated. Their parents wanted them to become responsible adults.

Traces of those "old school" virtues can be found in some private schools that David Hicks has guided. But Hicks is motivated by concepts of virtue and humanity that transcend social class or elite status. He is optimistic enough to challenge the leadership of these schools to restore educational norms—standards of morality and excellence—and nobility, to elevate students to lives of virtue and achievement. That is a worthy goal for any school setting, and it is the explicit goal of classical educators.

VI

Catholic Classicism

No institution has a longer tradition or more vigorous claim to classical education than the Catholic school. While only a few Catholic schools refer to themselves as classical, Catholic education has always contained a classical element, and today there are a variety of classical forms within the orbit of Catholic education, including home schools, home school co-operatives, parochial schools, and private schools. Though a relatively small movement, classicism has a long heritage and a natural home within Catholicism.

The roots of Catholic education are secured in the thought of the Church Fathers. Cassiodorus (c. 485-585) set up the first *scriptorium* in the sixth century to record what, even by his time, were the classics of antiquity. By the Middle Ages, Thomas Aquinas and other scholastics had worked out a sophisticated theory of the order of knowledge, providing for a careful integration of classical Greek and Roman writings into the Christian school. In the sixteenth century, Ignatius Loyola founded the Jesuit order, establishing what has become, through its schools, the largest religious institution in the Catholic world. When John Baptist de la Salle, a French priest, founded the Brothers of the Christian Schools in the late seventeenth century, he developed a strategy for teaching, designed a teacher's manual, and opened a school to train teachers. One might well regard him as the father of the modern school.

Elizabeth Ann Seton gave birth to the Catholic school system in the United States when she started a school for Catholic families in Emmitsburg, Maryland, in 1808. But the rapid growth of Catholic schools in the nineteenth century, spurred by a flood of immigrants, generated conflict with the dominant Protestant culture, which was enshrined in the government-run schools of the day.

Protestant reaction was severe and bore long-lasting consequences.

The 1834 burning of a Catholic convent in Charlestown, Massachusetts, and the 1844 Philadelphia Bible riots were dramatic events. But an attempt by the New York State legislature to halt state funding for Catholic schools was more significant. Following New York's lead, other states soon added amendments to their state constitutions, decreeing that public money could no longer be used to support educational institutions affiliated with religious denominations (and that even applied to the Protestant schools that had previously received government funding). This shortsighted decision led to increased restrictions on the role of religion in education in the twentieth century and may well have been the most influential educational decision of the last 150 years.[1]

Catholics responded to these funding decisions vigorously. Enrollment in Church-run schools increased from 500,000 students in 1884 to 2 million in 1920 and peaked at 5.6 million in 1965.[2] Most Catholic Irish in the mid-1800s were poor and semi-literate when they immigrated to America. But Catholics grew wealthier and integrated themselves into American culture, especially with rising prosperity after World War II. By 1960 an Irish Catholic was President.

But a crisis was brewing in Catholic education. Peter Hastings, a Catholic school head, broadly claims that before 1965 Catholic schools "appeared to be 'worshipping communities of faith' composed of believing, practicing Catholic staff and pupils. Their task was the transmission of a package of beliefs ... and of rules .... This was often transmitted by manipulation."[3] Hastings says this produced "moronic" religious thinkers and morally immature adults teaching in a closed school system.

The Second Vatican Council (1962-65) seemed to recognize at least some validity to this charge. Building on a 1929 encyclical *On Christian Education* by Pope Pius XI, the Council issued a Declaration of Religious Freedom, which stated that "Truth ... is to be sought after in a manner proper to the dignity of the human person and his social nature. The inquiry is to be free, carried on with the aid of teaching or instruction, communication and dialogue, in the course of which men explain to one another the truth they have discovered, or think they have discovered, in order thus to assist one another in the quest for truth."[4] It continues, "In spreading religious faith ... everyone ought at all times to refrain from any manner of action which might seem to carry a hint of coercion or of a kind of persuasion that would be dishonorable or unworthy."[5]

Such statements appeared to encourage Catholic educators toward a new openness. Indeed, Vatican II marks a turning point in American Catholic education. But the results have been very mixed. While the causes are difficult to identify and include demographic changes such as declining birth rates, Catholic education has experienced a precipitous decline since the mid-1960s. In 1965 over 13,000 Catholic schools enrolled more than 5.5 million students. But by 1989 nearly 5,000 schools had closed and the remaining ones enrolled only 2.5 million students.[6] Between 2000 and 2013, 2,090 schools closed or were consolidated (25.7%). The number of students declined by 651, 298 (24.5%) so that just over 2 million students remained enrolled in catholic schools. In 2013 the number of operating Catholic schools was half (6,685) the number open in 1965.[7]

Yet a ray of light persists. While some inner-city schools have closed due to a lack of resources and "white flight," many more remain open and, increasingly, minority parents of all faiths are turning to them. Between 1970 and 1989, the number of minority students enrolled in Catholic schools increased by over 100,000. In fact, in 1989, minority students constituted 23.3% of the total enrollment in Catholic elementary schools; in 2000 they made up 25.6%, and in 2010 the percentage had risen to 29.8%.[8]

The Cristo Rey Model

Today, one successful—and growing—model of Catholic high school in urban centers is the Cristo Rey ("Christ the King") Network, started in Chicago by the Rev. John P. Foley, S.J. Though not explicitly classical in their pedagogy, these schools provide valuable help for students by partnering with businesses that provide internships. The students spend one day a week interning, and the businesses contribute the students' "wage" to the school, significantly lowering the cost of education. There are currently 28 Cristo Rey schools in 18 states and the District of Columbia serving 9,000 young people who live in urban communities and have limited educational options. Across the network, students of color make up 96 percent of enrollment, with an average family income of $34,000. Two thousands businesses provide internships, and in 2012 the Walton Family Foundation pledged $1.6 million to open two dozen more Cristo Rey Schools that will serve an additional 10,000 young people.[9]

The composition of Catholic schoolteachers has changed as well. In 1965 most were members of religious orders, but by 1975 only a handful of instructors from religious orders remained. Lay teachers, most—but by no means all—Catholic, were educating Catholic children. This rapid transformation created a crisis of leadership whose outcome is still uncertain. In 2013-2014, only 3.2% of the professional staff members at Catholic schools were from religious orders or the clergy.[10]

Historically, Catholic schools have maintained some of the highest academic standards, and their students are regularly accepted to the most competitive colleges in the nation. But some schools seem to have drifted away from a close alliance with the doctrines and practices of the Catholic Church. Indeed, a recent criticism voiced by Catholic families directed toward many diocesan Catholic schools is that they are "not Catholic enough," a concern borne out in the 2011 Cardus Education Survey, which found that "the moral, social, and religious dispositions of Catholic school graduates seem to run counter to the values and teachings of the Catholic church." The study also discovered that Catholic schools seem to be "largely irrelevant" in the long-term faith of their students and are "sometimes even counterproductive to the development of their students' faith."[11]

The last 50 years have seen great changes in American Catholicism. Donna Steichen sums up these changes in the preface to the Catholic home-schooling guide, *Designing Your Own Classical Curriculum*: "Catholic culture reached its highest development within Western civilization," she says, "but in the past thirty years that culture ... has collapsed in a vast secularizing implosion." Catholics who intended to transmit their traditional beliefs to their children anticipated a battle with their enemies in modern society, but they also discovered opponents within the Church.

This matters greatly to Mrs. Steichen, but it does not mark the end of the story. She continues: "The old culture has vanished from most Catholic institutions, but it has not died. It is still alive in faithful Catholic families, not only those of aging believers who refuse to relinquish the past, but also in young families who are consciously reclaiming it. These young parents ... are doing what the monasteries did for Catholic culture in an earlier Dark Age—preserving it and passing it on."[12]

To grasp what's happening in these present-day "monasteries" in the home, and in some Catholic schools, one needs to consider the ideas underpinning Catholic education and the place of classical education within the tradition of Catholic education.

The Theory

Catholic educators ascribe a dual role to Catholic education. Education must first nurture the child, and then it must induct the child into the Church and her vast spiritual resources. The two are distinct only as ideas. In practice, they overlap and feed on each other.

These purposes enable Catholic educational theory to share much in common with classical theory. The Vatican's Sacred Congregation for Catholic Education says of the Catholic Church that "She establishes her own schools because she considers them as a privileged means of promoting the formation of the whole man, since the school is a center in which a specific concept of the world, of man, and of history is developed and conveyed."

In *The Holy See's Teaching on Catholic Schools*, Archbishop J. Michael Miller outlines five qualities of Catholic Schools. First, Catholic schools are inspired by a supernatural vision that sees Catholic education as "a process which forms the whole child, especially with his or her eyes fixed on the vision of God. The specific purpose of a Catholic education is the formation of boys and girls who will be good citizens of this world, enriching society with the leaven of the Gospel, but who will also be citizens of the world to come."[13]

Second, Catholic schools are founded on a Christian anthropology— a term that means "an understanding of man" and that comes from the Greek word for "man," *anthropos*. As Archbishop Miller quotes from a Vatican instruction, this anthropology "includes a defense of human rights, but also attributes to the human person the dignity of a child of God; it attributes the fullest liberty, freed from sin itself by Christ, the most exalted destiny, which is the definitive and total possession of God himself, through love. It establishes the strictest possible relationship of solidarity among all persons; through mutual love and an ecclesial community. It calls for the fullest development of all that is human, because we have been made masters of the world by its Creator. Finally, it proposes Christ, Incarnate Son of God and perfect Man, as both model and means; to imitate him, is, for all men and women, the inexhaustible source of personal and communal perfection."

Miller adds, "Having a sound anthropology enables Catholic educators to recognize Christ as the standard and measure of a school's catholicity, 'the foundation of the whole educational enterprise in a Catholic school,' and the principles of the Gospel as guiding educational norms."[14]

Third, Catholic schools must be animated by communion and community. The Holy See desires "the development of the school as a community" in three ways: "the teamwork or collaboration among all those involved; the interaction of students with teachers and the school's physical environment."[15] Parents must be involved in the education of their children, and the teacher's "rapport with the students ought to be a prudent combination of familiarity and distance." Teachers should be familiar enough with each student to engender trust, but also distant enough to encourage independence and the responsible exercise of freedom.

The physical environment of the school is important as well. "If Catholic schools are to be true to their identity, they should try to suffuse their environment with this delight in the sacramental. Therefore they should express physically and visibly the external signs of Catholic culture through images, signs, symbols, icons and other objects of traditional devotion." Good art which is not explicitly religious should also be evident.[16]

Fourth, Catholic schools should be imbued with a Catholic worldview—not a mere intellectual perspective, but a "comprehensive way of life." The Catholic school does not derive its distinctiveness from the quality of instruction, catechesis, or pastoral activities, but because it "undertakes to educate the whole person, addressing the requirements of his or her natural and supernatural perfection. It is integral and Catholic because it provides an education in the intellectual and moral virtues, because it prepares for a fully human life at the service of others and for the life of the world to come." Vatican documents do not prescribe the specifics of how to educate students in a Catholic school, but the Holy See does "provide certain principles and guidelines which inspire the content of the curriculum if it is to deliver on its promise of offering students an integral education."[17]

Two key principles are integral to Catholic education, particularly in overcoming what Pope Benedict XVI called the "'dictatorship of relativism'—a dictatorship which cripples all genuine education." First, the contemporary world needs to hear that truth is the "fundamental value without which freedom, justice and human dignity are extinguished" (Pope John Paul II, *Veritatis splendor*, 4). Second, church members should engage the culture in light of the Gospel. Catholic education seeks the synthesis of culture and faith. Students are to be taught to appreciate the "positive elements in culture and strive to help them foster the further inculturation of the Gospel in their own situation," but they must also learn to be critical. The Catholic faith provides the essential principles for critique and evaluation, while the Catholic school seeks to be a place where "faith, culture and life are brought into harmony."[18]

Fifth, the Catholic school should be sustained by the witness of teaching. Miller encourages Catholic schools to be "rigorists" about who they hire. He says that "principals, pastors, trustees and parents share ... in the serious duty of hiring teachers who meet the standards of doctrine and integrity of life essential to maintaining and advancing a school's Catholic identity .... The careful hiring of men and women who enthusiastically endorse a Catholic ethos is ... the primary way to foster a school's catholicity." Teachers must manifest a Christian witness because "children will pick up far more by example than by masterful pedagogical techniques, especially in the practice of Christian virtues."[19]

This glimpse at Catholic theory reveals it to be not only friendly to classical education, but to share its essential elements. These five characteristics of Catholic education mesh well with the four characteristics of classical education presented in this book, namely: a high view of man, logocentricity, a respect for the Western tradition, and a pedagogy that concentrates its efforts on a true classical liberal arts education.

Catholic education is rooted in a tradition that values a sense of history. To varying degrees, Catholic schools seek to understand their Western heritage. Too often modern educators speak of the individual's freedom to inquire but, by their rejection of guidance from tradition and history, they practice what Paideia has identified as "first column" didactic instruction. Catholic education bridges the gap between inquiry and tradition by following the same pattern that classical educator David Hicks prescribes: Dogma should be followed by dialectic engagement. The student uses critical thought and imagination to come to terms with knowledge grounded in history. The dialectic between the individual and the world is thus restored.

Catholic schools prioritize the liberal arts, emphasizing knowledge, thought, communication, and conversation. Here is a living expression of the trivium, even though it may not use the same language as Dorothy Sayers and the Association of Classical and Christian Schools or apply them in the same way. The great books serve as vessels of the great ideas. Virtue takes priority over power, character over career, wisdom over knowledge, and social responsibility—the duty of civic involvement stressed by David Hicks—takes precedence over an inordinate attention to individual rights.

Catholic schools promote personalism over individualism. They encourage warm relationships between teacher and student. Dialogue and collegiality are held out as ideals.

Convictions about the dignity of the child define Catholic theory and practice, and they set protective limits on how Catholic schools organize themselves and how teachers manage their classrooms. Catholic teachers believe in something and are not ashamed to say what they believe. Confident in their beliefs, they don't hesitate to place demands on their students.

The purpose of Catholic education as proclaimed by Pope Pius XI is "to cooperate with divine grace in forming the true and perfect Christian." This task "takes in the whole aggregate of human life, physical and spiritual, intellectual and moral...not with a view of reducing it in any way, but in order to elevate, regulate, and perfect it, in accordance with the example and teaching of Christ."[20]

The twentieth century produced many shattered philosophies of education that appeal only to the material or the natural, ignoring the psychological and spiritual. Ideologies that seemed to promise liberty and limitless growth have borne disappointing fruit. The modern school is prevented—by its own methods and presuppositions—from reaching the soul and spirit. Catholic education seeks to reestablish this contact, and the classical tradition provides a means to this end.

The Practice

Catholic schools implement classical theory in the curriculum in different ways because each school and diocese takes responsibility for the practice of Catholic education. But some of the richest sources of Catholic classical education can be found in the extensive network of Catholic homeschoolers. Laura Berquist led the way with *Designing Your Own Classical Curriculum,* an insightful and practical work on classical homeschooling first published in 1994. Berquist founded Mother of Divine Grace School in 1995, and it now serves about 4,000 students. It is accredited and licensed in California and provides home schooling legal and curricular assistance to families. Mother of Divine Grace helps home schooling families translate what they are doing at home into language that schools understand and appreciate. They maintain transcripts and provide testing, mentoring, and many other services to help parents competently teach their own children. St. Thomas Aquinas Academy, another independent private school in California, offers a 12-year Catholic liberal arts education to home schooling families. And the Angelicum Academy, discussed in the next chapter, brings Mortimer Adler's classical principles into the Catholic homeschool.

Saint Jerome's Catholic School in Hyattsville, Maryland, is a shining example of a Catholic school that has switched to an explicitly classical curriculum with encouraging results. It faced closure in 2009 if it could not increase student enrollment and become more financially stable. There were many Catholic families in the ethnically diverse community surrounding the parish, but they did not enroll their children because they did not feel that the school was teaching the beauty of the Catholic Church. St. Jerome's hired Mary Pat Donoghue as principal, and she commissioned a curriculum committee to imagine what the ideal Catholic school could be.

The committee envisioned a Catholic school that is thoroughly classical in its academic curriculum and thoroughly Catholic in its world view. This was a massive shift in focus for the school and not simple to implement, but the results have been overwhelmingly positive. The school is now much more financially stable and has grown by 16% since 2009. Ms. Donoghue says this change to a classical curriculum "reaches to the tradition and can be a lifeline to Catholic schools today if they will reach for it."

Wayside Academy in Peterborough, Ontario, a private Catholic school, has also transitioned to a classical curriculum. Their curriculum was created over the course of five years by an eclectic group, including high school teachers and home schooling mothers. The group included so-called "curriculum experts," but all involved were passionate about classical education. The curriculum they devised has been lauded and endorsed by an international order of the Catholic Church, the Institute of the Incarnate Word. Terrence Prendergast, the Archbishop of Ottawa, has also recognized Wayside Academy as not only "a place of learning, but ... also a centre of faith, a nucleus of culture, and a pole of the Christian community." He states that Wayside Academy adds "incomparable richness to the people of God in our land."[21]

Perhaps the most thoroughly classical of Catholic schools is found in northern California's Napa Valley. The Kolbe Academy, named after St. Maximillian Kolbe, the "saint of Auschwitz," opened its doors on September 8, 1980. It enrolled eight children from three families, ages 5 through 13 and spanning seven grades. Their parents wanted intensive basic education for their kids and opposed the sex education and "values clarification" classes typical of that time and place. On the first day of school the students met their teacher, Thomas Aquinas College graduate Theresa Moore, and began a journey in Catholic classical education.

Kolbe Academy is dedicated to developing the qualities of academic excellence, independent work habits, "a desire to seek and find," and the ability to reason, while it presents students with the treasury of Catholic faith.[22]

When Kolbe founder Francis Crotty retired as school administrator in 1999, he had good reason to be proud of his school's accomplishments. Kolbe Academy Day School had placed a limit of 60 students on its own enrollment. But its influence was growing. SCHOOL-START, a worldwide program, was helping to establish small private schools on the Kolbe model, and the Kolbe Home School Program was allowing over 500 home school students to follow the same curriculum as Kolbe students. The Kolbe School moved from a small Victorian house in San Jose to its own campus with 7,500 square feet of classrooms, an auditorium, and a 3,500 book library. Recently Kolbe Academy merged with Trinity Grammar and Prep to become Kolbe Academy/Trinity Prep, which educates students from pre-kindergarten through high school. The school has doubled in size to 120 students (47 in high school) and serves over 1,200 students via their home school forum.

Oral presentations are part of the wider culture of communication at Kolbe Academy. Teachers carefully discipline grammar school students in the basics of reading and writing. Middle and high school students participate regularly in speech, debate, and drama. This emphasis on communication comes from Kolbe's commitment to the Ignatian form of classical education, which stresses *eloquentia perfecta*, or effective communication. The high school students write frequently, three to four papers a quarter per subject, which translates to about ten papers a quarter total.

The whole Kolbe curriculum revolves around the principles of Ignatian education. Students are taught to speak, write, and live as true Catholics "with the consent of all [their] faculties." Students in the early grades lay a foundation in the basics, with a strong emphasis on memorization. Critical thinking is cultivated so that students are able to meet the intellectual challenges of the day. Character is nurtured through the education of the whole person, including training in such social graces as poise and courtesy. Students are prepared for the duties and responsibilities of citizenship. Because Ignatian education cultivates appreciation for great achievement, both artistic and spiritual, students encounter the great books as core elements of an integrated curriculum. Teachers emphasize the relationship between music and the visual and performing arts and literature.

Kolbe students study Latin starting in fifth grade and Greek starting in seventh. In high school, students can either continue in Latin or take Italian. Their history program begins with Bible history for kindergarten through third grade. Starting in fourth grade, students learn Greek history and early world history. The history program in the lower grades emphasizes the "four facts of history": places, dates, people, and events.

In high school "the classics determine the scope of the curriculum." Students study the immortal works of Homer, Virgil, Dante, and Shakespeare at their own level because Kolbe is convinced that the great books are accessible to the high school student, though in a manner and degree different from the adult. Believing in the unity of knowledge, Kolbe High School integrates courses through a matrix that approaches the subjects of knowledge through history. The high school offers a seminar program in which students study a topic separate from the curriculum. The discussion is to be influenced by what they have learned, not what they think about the topic. Students have to defend their position using the texts they have read. The seminar meets once a week. Students receive the topic a week in advance and have to come to the seminar with knowledge of the topic and ready to discuss it.

One consequence of this breathtaking curriculum is that students score 150 points higher than the national average on the SAT and have a nearly 100% graduation rate when they go to college.[23] In 1997, the only Kolbe graduate was a National Merit Scholar. In 2007, Kolbe had three National Merit Semi-finalists. Kolbe students have won numerous speech, spelling, writing, and geography contests.

Even so, the goal of Kolbe's curriculum is not to produce students who are more learned for learning's sake. The Kolbe curriculum is not for an elite student, but for the average student. And it is ordered to the higher calling of virtue and obedience. It is religious first and foremost, and it views classical education as a means to an end. Because it is for the kingdom of Christ, it stresses social responsibility. Ignatian instructors look to the words of Daniel 12:3 for inspiration: "They that instruct many to justice shall shine as stars for all eternity." As Father Walter Burghardt has said, Ignatian education "has never envisioned knowledge primarily as a perfection of one's self, always as a means of linking us with others .... Communication is not just oratory; it's community, communion."[24]

Even Kolbe's oral presentation is best viewed as practice for the spiritual life. Ignatian education promotes the principle of emulation. In dramatic performance the player wears a mask, which parallels the spiritual life, as C.S. Lewis explained in *Mere Christianity*. When a Christian turns from temptation he has put on a mask, acting as though sin did not interest him. Through continual wearing of the mask, the features of the wearer are gradually molded to match the mask. As one Kolbe instructor puts it, "Learning to wear the mask of charity ... is our spiritual work. The taking-on of roles in dramatic performance, therefore, is an exercise akin to that of the spiritual life. Acting can, when properly directed, bring one closer to the spiritual goal."[25]

The classical Catholic vision of Kolbe Academy has lead to academic and moral success. Yet, education has always been difficult and many Catholic schools are struggling. James Day suggests that much Catholic education is characterized by a "pedagogy of estrangement" which has led many students in Catholic schools and colleges to moral confusion. The moral curriculum becomes a formality that reminds students and their teachers of the gap that exists between their communities of concern. In this environment, students cannot be honest about their struggles or question teachings, and teachers do not know the students they instruct.[26]

But the Catholic school that fits Day's description is neither truly Catholic nor truly classical. Nor is it necessary. True Catholic education is fundamentally a moral education, though many students growing up in Catholic schools are not learning to be morally discerning men and women. This estrangement, however, is not unique to the Catholic school. The defensive, formalistic approach to morality and doctrine that is common to the evangelical school creates the same sort of dichotomy between public and private life, and between the soul and body of the student.

Classical education, rightly understood, is the pursuit of wisdom and virtue through the means described in this book. By including both tradition (Western, Catholic, or Protestant) and dialogue, classical education unlocks the gate separating students from their best selves by means of a liberal arts education that respects the Western tradition, recognizes the divine image in humanity, and asserts that the world makes sense and is knowable.

Christian educators must return to the classical tradition. They must teach the dogma and the tradition, both the divine and the human, and do so when students are young. When a student reaches the dialectic years and needs to ask questions and realize his own dignity and beliefs, educators must leave room for them to question the tradition. Most children do not want to abandon or destroy tradition. They want to test its sufficiency for their lives and identities. The classical approach provides a procedure that will allow them to explore the relationship between their ideals and their duties. It offers a roadmap to guide them as they grow into the rhetoric stage in which their integrated soul can voice conclusions they have drawn and in which they can bear witness with no dichotomy between their private and public lives.

Catholic education is driven by high and noble ideals, a breathtaking perception of humans and the cosmos they inhabit, and a pedagogy that follows from these ideals and perceptions. Some Catholic educators have never turned away from the classical tradition. Others are seeing anew what classical Catholic education can accomplish, especially in the home-schooling movement.

Rare is the Catholic school that opposes the classical vision we have espoused in this book; for classical education turns on the vision of what man is, of his responsibilities, and of the curriculum and method that follow from this vision. Classical education is a foundational curriculum. It includes classical languages; the great ideas developed in the humanities; the trivium of grammar, logic, and rhetoric as verbal arts; and the quadrivium of arithmetic, geometry, harmonics, and astronomy as mathematical arts. But as Catholics understand all too well, the content is not an end in itself. It is a "via," a path to wisdom and virtue for all educators, but especially for the Catholic educator whose tradition contains the inspiration of Irenaeus (c. 130-202), who stated long ago, "The glory of God is the human person fully alive."

VII

Liberating Classicism

One way of testing the mettle of classical education is to see how it addresses the extraordinary cases of schooling. The children of our nation's racial minorities and the poor living in urban areas are among the greatest casualties of our educational system. Many public school officials argue that schools can do little until the economic and social problems of the inner city are solved. Would a classical school do any better? America is a prosperous nation with a high standard of general learning, but how would classical education fare in foreign settings? And what about students with special needs? How can classical education work in the area of learning differences? What hope does classical education offer in these special circumstances?

Hope is what the modern inner city needs, and many in the classical education movement are seeking to bring it there. Dr. George Grant, for example, is a well-known speaker, writer, and entrepreneur. He began the King's Meadow Study Center in 1991 to help Christians develop a cultural expression of the Protestant and Reformed Christian worldview in art, music, literature, politics, social research, community development, and education. Dr. Grant has helped start a number of classical schools around America such as Franklin Classical School in Franklin, Tennessee, and several others in urban settings, including New Hope Academy in Franklin.

Former President George W. Bush visited New Hope Academy and said, "Right out here on the outskirts of Nashville, Tennessee, in Franklin, Tennessee, at New Hope Academy, ... where children from differing backgrounds study together, learn the classics together ... they are providing a vision for the children, a vision that is positive and optimistic and clear. It's one thing to teach a child to read, but we want the literate child to see a better day."[1]

Begun in 1996 and currently overseen by Mr. Stuart Tutler, the school currently has a K-6 program and plans to add 7th and 8th grades. Mr. Tutler acknowledges that finances are always a challenge, but their greatest challenge is educating their community on how to live together in understanding. Having such diversity in close proximity "causes a lot of uncomfortable but wonderful conversations," Tutler said.[2]

Students from New Hope, which does not have a high school, go on to many of the private schools in town, including the Franklin Classical School. Many of them have to qualify for scholarships and financial assistance, but "the best and most elite schools in town are beating down our doors for our students; they are just that high of quality," says Mr. Tutler.

The school assesses its success by going beyond the normal metrics of test scores, etc., to an evaluation of the quality of their relationships. They keep in close contact with their alumni, the oldest of whom are now finishing college and entering adult life. These former students are carrying forth the mission of the school into their careers and plans by choosing to serve their local community and invest in others' lives rather than focusing on their financial goals.

Another classical school with a mission oriented toward the disadvantaged is The Oaks Academy in Indianapolis, Indiana. The Oaks seeks to bring justice to what it sees as a black eye for both public and private education alike: that most schools "simply view children as potential college fodder."[3] Believing this to be a very low view of the child, The Oaks established their mission and name from a contemplation of Isaiah 61: "They will be called oaks of righteousness, a planting of the LORD for the display of his splendor. They will rebuild the ancient ruins and restore the places long devastated; they will renew the ruined cities that have been devastated for generations."

Since 1998 The Oaks has purposely set out to close the gap between those who are in low-income homes and those in the upper middle class by having classes that are evenly made up of such demographics. They are starting a second school to allow more children to take advantage of their offerings. They also plan to establish a school leadership residency program to train future school leaders. Their curriculum brings together elements from the Marva Collins School, ACCS materials, and Charlotte Mason.

The King's Meadow Study Center and The Oaks intentionally seek to follow Christ's mandate to take the truth out into the entire world, including students who are poor and needy.

Hope Academy in Minneapolis, Minnesota, serves as a great example of an inner-city urban school that has, from its beginnings, sought to bring healing and understanding to the divide between the classes of Minneapolis. The school's founder, Russ Gregg, and his wife began seeking where they would purchase their first home in the Minneapolis area in the 1990s. Hoping to be salt and light, they moved into the Philips neighborhood, the poorest part of Minneapolis with the highest crime rate in Minnesota. With over 100 different languages spoken in that neighborhood, it was one of the most ethnically diverse neighborhoods in the United States. Gregg was working in a suburban Christian school as its development director. As their children became school aged, he enrolled them in the school where he worked.

But as Gregg loaded up his kids and headed for school every day, they drove by the kids from their neighborhood waiting for buses. Driven by a desire to provide a better education for those children, Gregg quit his job and embarked on founding and opening Hope Academy in the Philips neighborhood in the fall of 2000.

Currently the enrollment at Hope Academy is about 400 students in K-12. Seventy-five percent of their student body comes from homes of poverty where most of the parents have not been graduated from high school. The high school graduation rate for that area is 30 percent. Ninety percent of the school's costs are underwritten by a sponsorship program in which people of means in the Minneapolis area agree to pay the tuition costs for a student at the school. Direct student-paid tuition covers the other ten percent.

Hope Academy's statement of vision expresses the heart of the school: "Believing that all children are created for God's glory and endowed by him with an inalienable potential to acquire wisdom and knowledge, Hope Academy covenants with urban families to equip their children to become the responsible, servant leaders of the 21st Century. Committed to the truth, discipline, and values of the gospel of Jesus Christ, Hope Academy pursues this aim by mobilizing educational, business, and community leaders towards the important goal of serving the youth of Minneapolis with a remarkable education, permeated with a God-centered perspective. This inter-denominational school will seek to unleash kingdom citizens who work for justice, economic opportunity, racial harmony, hope for the family, and joy in the community."[4]

When Gregg began Hope Academy, he wanted the school located in the Philips neighborhood, clearly Christian, classical, and available to all students from that community who wished to come. Starting out with the models of other classical Christian schools, Gregg knew an inner-city student body would require some adjustments. He was convinced, however, that the classical model would best suit the needs of his students. "I just could not settle on God wanting me to give less than 100 percent of what I wanted for my own children to those living around me."[5]

Gregg and his staff believe strongly that any student (from an urban setting or not) must not be relegated to a second-class education, but can be ennobled by a first-rate education that is rigorous. "There is no place for shoddy Christian education. We are preparing Minneapolis' next generation of leaders; therefore we must equip them with the core knowledge to take on the most demanding leadership roles required of the twenty-first century. An academically rigorous course of study will best prepare students to deal purposefully and responsibly with the complex issues of living in this present society."[6]

The curriculum of Hope Academy varies slightly from what you would expect to find in other classical schools. Built around the schema of Dorothy Sayers' essay, "The Lost Tools of Learning," the student is led through a set of developmental stages with an emphasis on writing skills. "From Kindergarten on, you will find our students listening to stories, reading aloud to one another, or reading silently at their desks. Throughout our entire elementary curriculum, our students begin mastering the writing process (pre-write, write, revise, edit) and learning strong writing skills by recognizing traits of effective writing (ideas, organization, word choice, sentence fluency, voice, and conventions). At every stage of a Hope Academy education, students participate in literature circles and reader's workshops—learning how to talk about a story and ask questions of a text."[7]

Hope Academy brings the affluent Christian leaders of Minneapolis into close contact with the poorest students in the city. The school wants both groups to learn about how to dwell together in understanding and community. By requiring student sponsors to be involved regularly in the lives of those they sponsor, the Christian community has to do more than simply give money to the urban school. They have to put faces with their support.

The Hope Academy model is defined by two basic community groups: the families and the staff. Every family is brought into the life and work of the school, and the faculty are drawn to Hope Academy by its mission. Consequently admissions and faculty hiring determine the culture and mission of the school. The school's families are often struggling financially, so bus transportation is provided free of charge to students living within the boundaries of Minneapolis. A hot lunch is available for all students and is also provided free of charge to those qualifying (currently about 75% of the student body). Hope Academy goes beyond simply teaching content to emphasizing character and discipline in its students. The school gives a great deal of time to educating the parents in how to develop a culture of learning in their homes and how to develop study skills in their students.

The selection of an excellent faculty that fully embraces the school's vision is a major consideration for Hope Academy. It is difficult to find teachers willing to work with disadvantaged children. The faculty that work together at Hope Academy study together, spend time together, and encourage one another in a true community of learning. The teachers have worked on their classical curriculum to ensure that it engages their students. In their study of history, African-American study is emphasized even as the students learn the full scope of Western history from ancient Egypt to American history through the Civil War. Math and science are both taught in a hands-on manner with a great deal of student inquiry. Latin is taught in 4th through 8th grades; high school students study Spanish. The fine arts are emphasized, and all students participate in art and music. The upper school curriculum is well-rounded, rigorous, and employs a rotating schedule that ensures all students receive the same material while allowing for smaller class sizes.

Though still a young school, Hope Academy's results are already evident through their reputation in the community, their high retention rates for both students and faculty, and their testing results. The community has embraced the school and the resulting high application rates challenge the school to stay true to its vision. Retention rates topping 90% for both students and faculty demonstrate that the vision of Hope Academy is producing an engaging community. Recent test scores highlight significant progress for Hope students: those living at or below the poverty level score about 40 percent higher in both reading and math than their peers at neighboring schools.

Of course, test scores are only a part of the overall culture of success to be found at Hope. Gregg emphasizes that the school looks as much at the character of their students as they do at their test scores. Though more difficult to measure, virtue is still a strong point of emphasis in the rigorous academic program. Hope Academy shines as a light in a dark place.

The school leads students to wisdom and virtue by holding them to strong academic standards and nurturing their souls with love and compassion. But keeping such a vision viable from both an economic and social perspective is difficult. More than one such school has closed its doors in recent years.

In the first two editions of this book, the story of Westside Preparatory School of Chicago (later renamed The Marva Collins Preparatory School) was told. Beginning in 1975, Westside stood in a rough neighborhood of Chicago, demonstrating the potential of what classical education can do in "the allegedly fetid ghetto." Despite the glowing press and vocal support of the community, Marva Collins Academy closed its doors in 2010. The statement released by Mrs. Collins stated that, "more parents are seeking alternatives to the $5,500 tuition, which has led to a steady decrease in funds."[8] With all the media attention and books that have been written on the success of Marva Collin's work, her model remains worthy of study. Her passion and vision resulted in many years of education in the midst of poverty, drugs, and violence in the Garfield Park area of Chicago.

A similar story can be found in pre-Katrina New Orleans. Since 1990, Desire Street Ministries has sought to inspire the Upper Ninth Ward of New Orleans with the Gospel of Christ and has always included educational endeavors as a part of its vision. Its Desire Street Academy opened in 2002, but Hurricane Katrina came through in 2005, forcing the school to move temporarily to the Florida panhandle. When the school was able to move back to New Orleans, so many former constituents had moved away permanently that the school was forced to close in 2010. Yet Desire Street Ministries' drive to see the poor of New Orleans educated continues in a new endeavor: founding classical charter schools. The Ministries' current leader is former NFL quarterback Danny Wuerffel.

Like Desire Street Academies, Great Hearts Academies of Phoenix, Arizona, has labored to plant classical charter schools in their area. Dan Scoggins, the CEO of Great Hearts, explains that their foray into Title I charter schooling has been a great success, resulting in 16 Phoenix-area schools started as of 2014. Great Hearts plans to take their model nation-wide, with more inner-city schools to come.

Great Hearts schools implement a core liberal arts curriculum, an academy ethos, small size, professionally diverse and uniquely qualified staff, visible leadership, and an involved set of parents. In their own words, they say this about their program:

Great Hearts offers the same academically rigorous program to all students and has no admissions criteria. Great Hearts professes a broad public commitment to provide a superior classical liberal arts education to all students who are curious and diligent .... The primary goal of Great Hearts Academies is to graduate thoughtful leaders of character who will contribute to a more philosophical, humane, and just society. To reach this goal, each student must freely discern his or her unique character and destiny during the program. Liberal education should bring each student to ask: what amongst the array of offerings and invitations spread before me in the future do I find meaningful? Graduates will then apply that confident self-understanding for a greater good beyond themselves.

Classical Education around the World

Classical Christian education is not just an American enterprise, and there are several examples of its success throughout the world. Dr. George Grant and the King's Meadow Study Center have established classical schools in Northern Iraq and Indonesia. The governments have been grateful for the efforts made to provide a quality education to their people.

The Medes School is a private, Christian, English-based network of schools operating in the secure Kurdish region of Northern Iraq. Dr. Grant sums up this effort: "We now have three thriving schools in Northern Iraq, 27 in Indonesia, 2 in Egypt, one in Jordan, and many more in the planning stages. God's grace abounds. There are always challenges when working in the Muslim world. And in the case of Indonesia and our efforts to get going in Korea and China, there is the added element of East versus West. But the good news is that classical Christian education is so robust and effectual, that we've been able to overcome the obstacles fairly gracefully. That doesn't mean it has been easy—anything but. And yet, the Lord has been so faithful to bless even our most meager efforts."[9]

The program began in response to requests from local church and government authorities to establish a school with English-based curriculum and international training support as a means to educate their children. On-site American teachers typically teach one or two courses per semester, with the balance of their time spent in relationships with students, their families, and community contacts. All curriculum development, international staffing, and training are coordinated through Servant Group International.

Over 95 percent of the students come from Kurdish Muslim families, with the remainder from Orthodox Christian, Evangelical Christian, and other backgrounds. Many students are children of local government officials and community leaders.

Special Needs Students

Not only is location (such as in inner cities or foreign lands) something that classical education is well suited to overcome, but different types of learners as well. Several efforts have been launched to apply the principles of classical education to special needs students. Veritas Christian Academy, in Fletcher, North Carolina, has implemented "School Within a School Support Systems," a model that seeks to mainstream students with special needs into the experience of a classical school while allowing them to receive the additional help they may need.

Begun in 2000, School Within a School was started to meet the needs of high-functioning Asperger's Syndrome students whose parents desired a classical education for their children. The program has since expanded to address other learning differences. Students who qualify for the program must have a minimum 90 I.Q., proper referrals, and be willing to take the entire normal course load with few exceptions. The School Within a School Support System aims to foster skills needed for a productive and independent life in the school, home, and community. These skills typically fall into the following categories:

Social and Life Skills, such as conversation skills, curiosity about others, and appropriate reactions to situations. Practical life skills such as problem solving, self-care and money management are also addressed.

Academic Support, including fluency in reading, reading comprehension, or the ability to stay on task when working.

Organizational Skills, including developing systems of organization for recording assignments, collecting needed materials, and breaking down large projects into manageable steps.

Study Skills, such as note-taking, test-taking, study strategies, goal-setting, time and task management, and homework/project planning.[10]

This program has continued to experience growth; it grew from serving just 10 students in 2010 to 26 students (or about 10 percent of their student body) in 2013. It emphasizes having the right teachers in place who have advanced training in learning needs and in building close working relationships between the staff in the Support system and the regular faculty.

2 12 212212121# # # # # # # # ## ## ##

The curriculum and methods are culled together by the faculty through their own research and experience, including such programs as Orton-Gillingham Multi-Sensory Education, Lindamood-Bell Learning Processes, Precision teaching and principles of Applied Behavior Analysis, and Social Thinking curriculum by Michelle Garcia Winner, and others. Special needs are assessed within one of five tiers of support, each tier adding additional tuition fees to the normal fee in return for additional services rendered by the School Within a School. Additional funds come from fundraising events.

The Director of the School Within a School says, "The goal is to have the student able to experience as much of the normal classroom experience and content while receiving the added help their special needs require. Classical education makes demands of all students, so mainstreaming students with special needs in this setting requires a lot of coordination. The support staff work very closely with the faculty. Our biggest challenge is finding the additional time a student needs for their support without robbing them of important classroom time. We continue to learn and apply what we learn to become better."[11]

Some schools choose to use classical methods in a stand-alone Special Needs School environment where obstacles to coordination are less prevalent. Dr. Paula Flint founded Flint Academy, in Arlington, Texas, because she wanted to provide for special needs children within the philosophies of Charlotte Mason and other classical education thinkers. In addition to beginning her study of classical education in the 1980s, she earned her Masters and Ph.D. in Special Education, and taught Special Education at the University of North Texas. Flint Academy opened in 2006 and is working to expand.

Flint Academy builds on some basic principles derived from Charlotte Mason and ACCS theory. Dr. Flint explains:

"We believe that God created each child unique and eternally significant with special gifts and talents. It is our job to help the child discover and develop those gifts and talents, so that the child may be equipped to serve God .... We should study, and teach our children to study, both God's world and the Holy Scriptures in order to understand His creation and to learn to know God and understand the relationship among His physical creation, the history of man, and the continuous thread of Christianity, thus developing a Christian worldview. To this end, we will provide an exemplary education in the classical disciplines of grammar ... logic ... and rhetoric ... in all subjects, so that each child may reach his full God-given potential and develop both the tools and the love for lifelong learning. We will be open to investigating and utilizing innovative educational ideas and the latest research in the field of education without succumbing to fads or sacrificing the classical goals of education. We also desire to educate those children with special needs, specific learning disabilities, and other potentially handicapping conditions as the Lord gives us wisdom, so that they also may reach their full potential and be able to accomplish what God has planned for them. No child shall be turned away from enrollment in The Flint Academy because of his or her disability or behavior, as long as the parents are willing to work with the school."[12]

Such a philosophy has led the school to several unique practices. The school day runs from 9:30 a.m. till 3:30 p.m., Monday through Thursday, with no homework, and Fridays are devoted to family time. The faculty uses the Friday schedule to develop individual educational plans, prepare lessons and materials, and attend teacher training meetings. Each classroom has one teacher and one aide, and a maximum of 12 students. If possible, the student will have the same teacher for two consecutive years. Diagnostic-prescriptive teaching is employed for all students and class grade-level designations are somewhat relaxed, though Flint Academy makes sure that any student wishing to move back into a more structured grade-level system will be able to do so. A strong culture of parental involvement and parent training permeate the school. Flint Academy also conducts itself as a laboratory research school, seeking to find best practices and introducing new approaches and materials as appropriate.

The classical strategies at Flint Academy resemble those of other schools using the classical model; they are simply applied to students with learning disabilities. Students at Flint begin Latin instruction in the 3rd grade, read only classical literature, use the Lost Tools of Writing, teach history and literature in a humanities framework, use primary source materials rather than textbooks, and study philosophy and logic in their high school. Students study and imitate great artwork, copy paintings "to learn respect for the artists and how much work is required, which frees the students up to try hard things."[13]

No grades are given to students; if they do poorly on something, they try again until the skill is mastered. Having two teachers in a room with only 6-12 students is the foundation of the school's success. If one student doesn't understand a concept, one of the teachers can talk with that student and give private instruction while the group moves forward. This system of having a teacher flow through the room and work individually is difficult (notes must be kept on each student) but effective. "Every teacher has to get every child to learn everything. Flint Academy changes the system for the students, rather than changing the students for the system."[14]

Classical Homeschooling

Homeschooling parents can also provide a classical education to their children. Cheryl Swope, in *Simply Classical: A Beautiful Education for Any Child*, tells the story of classically teaching her daughter, Michelle, who has been diagnosed with both autism and schizophrenia, among other disabilities. Part memoir, part manual, Swope's book provides heartwarming and convincing help for parents of special needs children. Swope asks, in the preface of her work, "If classical education could give Helen Keller the tools to overcome great obstacles and embrace the 'sweeps of the heavens' so many years ago, why do even less-severely challenged special-needs children fail to receive such a bountiful classical education today?"[15]

The diversity expressed in this chapter's schools and efforts make clear that classical education fits a broad array of special needs, geographical locations, and unique situations. The challenge lies in helping more people see its flexibility, overcoming financial needs, and strengthening the culture of learning in some places. The compassionate folk who labor in these works see that the respect inherent in the classical model brings hope to families who have unusual circumstances, just as it does to all parents who truly wish to educate their children.

VIII

Classical Homeschooling

Many Americans believe that reforming education requires bringing parents back into a place of responsibility and involvement in their child's education. The homeschool movement plays a vital role in this effort. In 1999, 850,000 American children were homeschooled. In 2003, this number had grown to 1.1 million children and, in 2007, there were 1.5 million homeschoolers. As of 2012 (the most recent data available), 1.77 million children were being homeschooled in the United States, more than doubling the number since 1999.[1] Heather Shirley, CCO of Classical Conversations, reports, "Parents are getting less and less enchanted with conveyor-belt education, and are more and more open to an education that is not anxiety driven."[2] Home education has begun a grassroots reformation from which there is no turning back. In this chapter we will explore the two main forms of home education: homeschooling and home-centered schooling.

Homeschooling is often no more than a parent who schools the family's children in the home with no formal outside involvement in that education. Parents teach their children, design the scope of study, produce or purchase the materials used, and generally lead their child's education. Depending on the state requirements, parents may have to report to the state for truancy laws, but their own convictions determine the over-all choices made in educating their child, usually with regular input from older students.

Home-centered learning is the same in many ways, with the exception of external influences. Many busy parents today are finding ways to homeschool by making use of services offered to them by various publishers, online academies, and cooperatives, where time is scheduled for joint study among several families, led by a parent skilled in the area of study. Online options function in much the same manner, with students around the nation signing into a course and studying together with a teacher. For the demanding courses studied in high school, many families are even making use of local community colleges and other educational supplements to provide an education that is still mainly conducted in the home.

History of American Homeschooling

Homeschooling has roots in ancient Hebrew and Roman education, and continued as a dominant model of education for thousands of years. In fact, prior to 1852, when compulsory education was introduced into America through a Massachusetts law,[3] the majority of education in America was performed within the walls of the family home. But homeschooling seems new to us because since the mid-1850s Americans have been encouraged to think about education in an institutional setting. But for roughly 2 million American children, that is no longer the case.

Homeschooling attracts parents because they see evidence that home-schooled students outperform students in private and government-run schools. A Homeschool Legal Defense Association study entitled, *Progress Report 2009: Homeschool Academic Achievement and Demographics*, conducted by Dr. Brian Ray of the National Home Education Research Institute, surveyed 11,739 homeschooled students for the 2007–08 academic school year, and showed that homeschoolers, on average, scored 37 percentile points above public school students on standardized achievement tests. Education News reports, "Homeschooling statistics show that those who are independently educated typically score between the 65th and 89th percentile on such exams, while those attending traditional schools average on the 50th percentile. Furthermore, the achievement gaps, long plaguing school systems around the country, aren't present in the home-schooling environment. There's no difference in achievement between sexes, income levels, or race/ethnicity."[4] Additionally, home education is proving to be quite cost effective, particularly when compared to public schools. The average public school spends nearly $10,000 per child per year whereas the Progress Report shows that the average homeschool parent spends about $500 per child per year.[5]

Even though their children do well academically, many parents say this is not why they school their children at home. Parents with a strong sense of responsibility for raising their children will naturally desire academic success, but these parents also see learning in relation to morality and character, qualities that cannot be directly measured and whose effects appear only over a long period of time. The evidence for the moral success of homeschooling must be anecdotal, but the most common observations are that homeschooling students tend to be more respectful to adults, more polished in the way they present themselves, more knowledgeable about learning and life, and more orderly in their conduct.

After 25 pioneering years of growth, experiment and study, homeschooling has come into its own. A September 2000 *Time* magazine article reported that, "Homeschooling's first wave of graduates is coming of age." There is even a college particularly designed for home-schooled students: Patrick Henry College in Purcellville, Virginia. But established colleges— even elite schools like Stanford and Harvard—also make room for homeschoolers. This wasn't always the case. "When homeschoolers were applying to college in the early '90s, the schools didn't know what to make of them," says Cafi Cohen, 50, who taught her two children at home and wrote *Homeschooling the Teen Years*. "Now most colleges have a policy for dealing with them, and some schools are just about rolling out the red carpet."[6]

Homeschooling has sometimes been characterized as a separatist movement or a withdrawal from American culture. But in reality it is a movement with great purpose and strong internal support. Parents who homeschool are aided by magazines such as *Homeschooling Today*, and by books, web sites, curriculum developers and reviewers, support groups and loops, and hundreds of local homeschool co-ops and networks. Susan Wise Bauer, who with her mother co-wrote *The Well-Trained Mind*, one of the most popular homeschool guides, writes that "My mother struggled hard to give us the benefits of a classical education. She began to teach us at home in a day when few materials existed for home-educating parents; she had to create her own curriculum." But those days are gone, observes Bauer, who explains that her and her mother's book will describe the much larger homeschool landscape that now exists: "We're going to lay out a whole plan of study for you—not just theory, but resources and textbooks and curricula."[7]

Homeschool freedom and experimentation contrast sharply with government school systems where progressive educational theories are institutionalized and restrict new developments. Groups seeking radical change, like the Paideia Group (see chapter 4), report tremendous resistance from professional administrators, teachers, and theorists. Homeschooling parents, by contrast, provide their own household administration while they focus on teaching. Indeed, over the past 25 years perhaps no group has gained more knowledge about education than the mothers of homeschooling families. By direct experience they have developed their own theories of learning and then taken them back into the classroom, receiving immediate feedback. They learn grammar, math, languages, and writing to teach their own children. They join support groups and meet on the web; they share resources and experiences; they treat education as the highest priority of childhood itself.

Seriousness about education, combined with rapid feedback on results, has naturally led homeschooling parents to discover classical education. Homeschooling's emphasis on responsibility and leadership inevitably includes a concern for virtue, and an emphasis on careful reasoning leads to education in logic, rhetoric, and debate. Homeschooling's stress on language skills prompts training in grammar and rhetoric. A parent who is used to rapid feedback quickly learns how well the child understands the lesson. Parent-teachers develop an intuitive awareness of the lesson's trivium. They become aware of the stages of growth—and thus aware of the trivium of the stages of life—by continually interacting with the child. A parent willing to teach her children demonstrates to them the love of learning, and this leads to the reading of good and great books. The increased time spent reading together leads both parent and child to want to find the best books. In short, more than two decades of homeschooling trial and error has prepared home educators to embrace something like the classical theory of education.

Charlotte Mason

The first clear model for homeschooling method to arise in America dates back to Charlotte Mason's writings and disciples. Charlotte Mason was a British educator and school reformer who lived from 1842 until 1923. She wrote a six-volume series that explains her educational philosophy and methods.[8] A survey of her methods and ideas, which are applicable to either a traditional classroom or the homeschool, was written by Susan Schaeffer Macaulay in 1984, entitled, *For the Children's Sake*.[9] This book brought the Charlotte Mason ideals back into popular use, especially among the home-school community. There are now a large number of resources online to help those who wish to pursue her ideas in their homeschool, in addition to conferences and workshops held around the country. Notably, Ambleside Schools hosts an online academy which provides free access to all Mason's writings and even modernizes them for greater accessibility.[10]

In its basic form, Charlotte Mason's view of education focuses on a three-pronged approach to the whole student. The motto of the Parents' National Educational Union which she founded was, "Education is an Atmosphere, a Discipline, [and] a Life." Mason believed that a child needs an engaging, loving, and alive atmosphere in order to become a life-long learner. She also believed that inculcating the habits of learning not only helped children mature into adulthood but also enabled them to become lifelong learners. This was the discipline she called for. And finally, she admonished the teacher to connect learning to life, not simply convey cold facts.

Mason emphasized teaching ideas along with the knowledge necessary to understand and embody them. "She thought children should do the work of dealing with ideas and knowledge, rather than the teacher acting as a middle man, dispensing filtered knowledge."[11] Her curriculum pushes for first-hand exposure to great and noble ideas through books, hands-on observation, and the enjoyment of art, music, and poetry. "The knowledge of God, as found in the Bible, is the primary knowledge and the most important. History is taught chronologically, using well-written history books, source documents and biographies. Literature is taught along with history, using books from or about the same time period. Language arts skills are learned through narration, which consists of the child telling back a story, first orally and later in written form; copy work, or the transcribing of a well-written piece of literature; and dictation of passages from their books. Memorization was used by Charlotte Mason not so much to assimilate facts, but to give children material to meditate or 'chew' on, so her students memorized scripture and poetry."[12]

Other characteristics of the Mason method include lessons at an age-appropriate length, usually short (15 minutes) for young children. The object was to gain complete focus on the subject at hand, while recognizing that young children could only do so for a short period of time. The lesson length would grow with age, a practice in sharp contrast with modern classroom practice, which makes little effort to develop attentiveness in students. She also emphasized the use of "living" books over textbooks, believing young minds would be stirred and engaged much more by well-written literature than by the fact-oriented texts present in most classrooms. Another trait of Mason's curriculum is the Nature Walk, an effort to see the student out and about in the world rather than kept to the sterile classroom. Nature was much more engaging and a great place to develop the habit of observation, which was key in the habits Mason emphasized.

Mason was popular at a time (the turn of the twentieth century) when classical education was fighting for its life against the newer views of progressive education. She was clearly seeking to hold on to the best of the past while also embracing the need to prepare students for life in a changing world. She strongly believed that emphasizing the soul, the heart of the student, would produce persons who could learn in any context. Her teachings were widely embraced both in Britain and America. Those educating at home found it even easier to use her methods than the teacher in the classroom facing 25 students at once. In the 1980s, when home-schooling was experiencing a renewal and classical education was also on the rise, it was natural that many would recover Mason's views, especially in the homeschool community. Her writings on education are currently in print, and numerous books and anthologies have been published on how her work can be used in our day.

Mason's approach is well within the pale of classical education: holding a high view of man, a logocentric approach (belief in knowable truth), devotion to Western civilization, and a curriculum that embodies those principles.

Susan Wise Bauer

Mrs. Bauer's book on classical education, *The Well-Trained Mind*, first appeared in 1999 and is now in its third edition. It sets forth some basic theory on how to homeschool classically, and then maps out a full kindergarten through twelfth-grade program of study. With this book as the center piece, Bauer has continued to develop materials that augment this program, including a series of books designed to be a narrative world history. Homeschooled by her mother, Susan has in turn taught her own four children at home. She has earned an M.A., M.Div., and Ph.D., and teaches at the College of William & Mary in Virginia. She now spends most of her time developing materials and speaking at homeschool conferences, while maintaining one of the largest online forum boards for the home-school movement.

The very structure of *The Well-Trained Mind* emphasizes the tools of learning outlined by Dorothy Sayers. In a prologue Jessie Wise (Susan's mother) briefly describes her experience as a parent raising children during what she later recognized were the stages of the trivium, and Susan offers a "personal look," describing what it was like to receive a classical education from her mother. In the introduction that follows, the authors promise to acquaint the reader with the Trivium and provide a 12-year plan to carry out a classical education. The Bauers then divide their book into four parts. The first three organize teaching by the stages of grammar, logic, and rhetoric, while the fourth describes how to bring the trivium into the homeschool.

Over the next 700 pages Jessie and Susan fulfill their commitment. Their book provides a thorough description of how to apply the trivium at home, including a careful explanation of the three stages of the child's development, an introduction to the keynote class for each stage—grammar, logic and rhetoric—guidance on how to accomplish class core goals, and a guide to each subject in the stage, including instructions on how to teach it, descriptive examples, and lists of recommended resources.

Throughout, Wise and Bauer develop a complete theory of the trivium. They refer to "the classical theory of education, which organizes learning around the maturing capacity of the child's mind." This maturing capacity means, "If grammar-stage learning is fact-centered and logic-stage learning is skill centered, than rhetoric-stage learning is idea-centered." The strength of classical theory is the way it identifies the stages of maturity and links them to corresponding learning activities. The authors explain that "The three part process of memorization, logical organization, and clear expression put [the classically educated students] far above their peers."[13]

Wise and Bauer distinguish between subjects best learned through repeating cycles and those subjects in which learning is progressive. They therefore propose two different class sequences over the stages of the Trivium. Cyclical classes such as history and science follow a pattern of four-year rotation: the student repeats a subject matter area every four years, but studies it in a manner that corresponds to his age and stage of development. Progressive classes such as math or grammar are studied in sequence, with the mode of study adapted to the student's place in the Trivium.

So, for instance, the history/geography cycle begins with a study of the "ancients" in first grade, and then continues through medieval-early Renaissance, late Renaissance-early modern, and modern over the next three years. The sciences follow a roughly corresponding cycle: biology in first grade, then earth science and astronomy, chemistry, and physics. This first cycle occurs at the grammar stage, where the focus is on memorization and knowledge of facts. The cycles begin again in fifth grade and ninth grade, corresponding to the appropriate stage: logic emphasizes explanatory thinking, while rhetoric emphasizes understanding of ideas and persuasive expression. After describing each subject, Wise and Bauer provide a time schedule and an extensive resource list.

The grammar stage from first to fourth grade is about collecting information. Wise and Bauer reiterate this point repeatedly. "A classical education requires a student to collect, memorize, and categorize information …. The first four years are the most intensive for fact collecting." The parent's role, then, is "to supply the knowledge and skills that will allow your child to overflow with creativity as his mind matures." This is reasonable because "the elementary years are ideal for soaking up knowledge." Furthermore, "The immature mind is more suited to absorption than to argument." And besides, "Most young children enjoy repetition and delight in the familiarity of memorized words." In short, "The key to the first stage of the curriculum is content, content, content."[14]

The parent's task is to serve as a source of information, to fill children's imaginations with images and concepts, pictures and stories, to "spread knowledge in front of them, and let them feast." Not to feast randomly, however, for the grammar stage develops essential skills. Wise and Bauer urge parents to prioritize reading, writing, grammar, and math in the grammar years. Classical education teaches a child how to learn, and reading is particularly important because classical education places great weight on the written word, but parents do not have to become "experts" in the subject matter they teach.

Because language is important, the parent/teacher should use grades one through four to make its proper use second nature to the child. The logic and rhetoric stages require the student to use language to reason, argue, and express ideas, but the student must first learn how to read, write, and speak. The student should also learn to spell and recognize the elements of English grammar. In a similar way, four years of grammar-level math prepare students for the higher levels of abstract thinking they will need to study algebra, trigonometry, and calculus.

Wise and Bauer's skills approach to classical education is clear when they assert: "Latin is not the defining element of a classical education. Classical education has to do with setting up solid foundations, with learning how to learn, with mental discipline and intellectual curiosity and a willingness to grapple with the lessons of the past. All of this is much more important than a single foreign-language course." Of course, "You still have to take Latin."[15] The authors echo Douglas Wilson, a founder of the Logos

School, in explaining how the study of Latin helps students, and they show parents how to teach it.

By fifth grade the student is ready for the logic stage. While homeschoolers in the elementary years perform higher on standardized tests than their public and private school counterparts, the differences become more marked in the middle school years. Wise and Bauer explain this widening gap when they introduce the middle, or Logic, stage in *The Well-Trained Mind.* "Somewhere around fourth grade," they suggest, "the growing mind begins to switch gears .... The mind begins to generalize, to analyze—to develop the capacity for abstract thought."[16]

Around the idea of what Wise and Bauer call "The Argumentative Child," they build their theory of the logic stage. Now the student begins to connect the data she has learned, to find relationships among them. "Now," they point out, "it's time for critical thinking." Critical thinking builds on and is dependent on the fact gathering of the grammar years, and parents should make sure to blend both presentation of the facts and logical examination of them.

Wise and Bauer provide instructions to show parents how to teach their middle schooler to evaluate arguments and trace connections between facts. The teaching process changes, no longer simply providing information; the teacher becomes the guide in a dialogue about ideas that children seek in original sources. The student needs supervision but rapidly grows independent and efficient.

Logic-stage teaching differs, and so does the material covered. Formal logic is taught, and logic trains the mind to seek out patterns and relationships, thus altering every subject. Language study focuses on syntax, "the logical relationships among the parts of a sentence." The student learns to *analyze* language. She is prepared for literary criticism by talking about what she reads with her parent, discussing plots, characters, and moral effects. Writing is studied formally.

Mathematics progresses to relationships between numbers. Science equips the child with a basic knowledge, but now the student begins to make connections between the branches of science, and between science and other areas of study. Reports and experiments dominate logic-level science as the student repeats the four-year cycle from her grammar school years.

History, too, moves beyond names, dates, and places, and becomes a way to find connections between events. The student repeats the four-year cycle of the grammar years, using tools like time-lines, outlines, a history notebook, and original sources to examine the motives of leaders, relationships between cultures, forms of government, and the application of morals to human action.

Art and music are coordinated with history so that the student learns about social and cultural developments and how they affect works of art. The logic-stage student may not perform in or produce the fine arts, but he will participate and develop an appreciation for the arts.

The child who progresses through the four years of middle school understands the structure of knowledge and can see the relationships between the various domains of learning. Furthermore, she is ready for rhetoric. Rhetoric is the capstone of the trivium. Because basic skills have been mastered, they need not be studied as specific subjects. These skills will not fade because, once she has acquired them, the student begins to use them. The rhetoric stage stresses expression and flexibility, training the student to write and speak on any curricular subject. The study of rhetoric is both the keynote and the controlling influence of the stage.

During this stage the student's personal interests and ability lead him to specialize. While grammar is studied through twelfth grade because few students will master it before finishing high school, other subjects can take a lower priority. In her "Lost Tools" essay, Dorothy Sayers says, "Those who are likely never to have any great use or aptitude for mathematics should be allowed to rest, more or less, upon their oars."

The rhetoric stage seems to have two keynotes: the formal study of rhetoric and the study of great books. The student evaluates texts, traces the development of ideas, and compares philosophies and movements to each other. History and literature, being closely related, are studied as one subject. The great books help the student reach the goal of the rhetoric stage, which Wise and Bauer describe as "a greater understanding of our own civilization, country, and place in time, stemming from an understanding of what has come before us."[17] They propose a list of books, but warn that lists are dangerous and must remain flexible, advising that books be read when students study the historical period in which they were written.

To read great books, the student must be taught advanced reading techniques. Instead of a formal writing class, the student should write about ideas and the contents of subjects. In both history/literature and the sciences, the rhetoric stage again repeats the four-year cycle of study.

Science, like all classical subjects, makes demands on the student to explore its own implications as well as to learn about the world. The three elements of the rhetoric-stage science program are the study of scientific principles, primary scientific source-readings, and an annual science paper. The rhetoric stage in the study of science enables the student to engage in the great conversation about science.

Wise and Bauer have little to say about math in the rhetoric stage; they simply present programs. But they do assert that basic literacy demands a competency in higher-math skills. They repeat Sayers' advice: "Most classical educators suggest that students who have no particular bent for mathematics and no plans for a career in science be allowed to 'rest on their oars' after completing basic upper-level mathematics requirements." Math requirements are met by tenth grade. In the junior and senior years, Wise and Bauer say math may be studied as an elective.

Rhetoric-level foreign language study pursues two goals: the college-prep requirement and mastery of one foreign language (while beginning high-school level study of a second foreign language). Students of art and music at the rhetoric level will have learned their conventions and, like words, will use them as forms of expression to convey ideas.

During the junior and senior years students focus on great books, science, art and music, and choose an elective in math, science, or language. The senior caps her high school career by completing a major writing project in a particular field of interest. The writing project may be rooted in one subject, but it will necessarily deal with ideas from all the subjects in the curriculum.

Wise and Bauer again provide resources and describe teaching methods for each class at the rhetoric stage. Their work meets a need and fulfills its promises. No other book provides a more detailed description of the trivium and how to apply it to the stages of a child's growth. *The Well-Trained Mind* has created a happy marriage of classical education and home-schooling, a relationship that has certainly met with Susan Wise Bauer's approval: "A classical education is worth every drop of sweat—I can testify to that. I am constantly grateful to my mother for my education. It gave me an immeasurable head start, the independence to innovate and work on my own, confidence in my ability to compete in the job market, and the mental tools to build a satisfying career."[18]

Classical Conversations

More than one mom, however, has picked up Bauer's large work and wondered, "How is one person to do all that work? Above all the dishes, housework, and other domestic duties, how can a mother become a curriculum developer, lesson planner, and book aficionado?" This feeling of being overwhelmed has moved many from strictly homeschooling into what is referred to as home-centered schooling, where a local community or online resource provides help and guidance as parents seek to teach their own children. One example of this option is the work of Classical Conversations.

Classical Conversations seeks to help develop home-centered education by forming local learning communities of various age groups, categorized into various levels of study that follow Sayers' model of child development. Most of the learning occurs in the home, but weekly meetings bring accountability and tutorial help to the students of local families who are members of a Classical Conversations learning group. Membership fees gain the member access to online resources, a teacher's guide, and the weekly meetings. The weekly meetings are locally organized and led. Classical Conversations provides support and guidance, with training for the local leadership as a group is formed.

Starting with her reading of Dorothy Sayers' "Lost of Tools of Learning" in 1996, Dr. Leigh Bortins, the founder of Classical Conversations, began putting together local communities that use her resources and materials to form classical home education groups across America. Starting in North Carolina, this organization is rapidly growing into the largest formal program for home-centered learning. Dr. Bortins began by working with her own children in a classical method based upon Dorothy Sayers' explanation of the trivium. When others expressed interest in her passionate descriptions of her own family's work, she developed a program so others could share in her joy.

Classical Conversations was formed to meet the needs of parents who seek a high-quality rigorous education for their children, but who desire help and resources. Because so few of today's parents received a classical education in their youth, many of those parents who now want to classically educate their children need help to do so, and Bortins saw an opportunity to assist them. Local groups were established, supported online and by regional training, and a systematic approach to classical home-centered learning developed.

Parents assign daily work to their student, to be augmented and added to at the weekly meeting, which is led by a local tutor trained by Classical Conversations in their methods and program. "Students enjoy their community of friends on the same journey; they encourage one another in their studies."[19] Because all the parents have been following the same *Curriculum Guide* from Classical Conversations, the weekly meetings can bring them together for unified study and tutorial help. The plan for kindergarten through twelfth grade takes the student through three sequential programs of study.

At a typical weekly meeting, which lasts 3-6 hours depending upon the age of the students, a trained tutor leads a small group (never more than 12 students) through a review of what they have covered the previous week and introduces the coming week's study. Held at a local meeting place large enough to accommodate all the students in all levels at once, the meetings aim to have families with multiple children come together and encourage one another in their studies. This allows older, more advanced students to help younger or struggling students. Each level of program follows the trivium developmentally, much as Dorothy Sayers set forth in her essay.

Classical Conversations offers its Foundations program for students in K4 up to 6th grade. Its main emphasis is the grammar activity of memory. In addition to absorbing facts from a number of subject areas that are learned through rhyme and song, and constantly reviewed, the student also practices public speaking, investigates science projects, and completes an art or music project each week. They then can stay and enjoy play and friendship if their older siblings have class after lunch.

Classical Conversations Essentials program applies the dialectic stage to students in the 4th through 6th grades. Meeting after having Foundations in the morning, (and then lunch), this afternoon experience allows for the tutors to model the grammar and dialectic tools of learning in English grammar, writing, and math drills. Students develop the mental skills to sort and classify facts and learn the tools they need to become effective writers.

The highest level is called the Challenge program. First there are the Challenge A & B levels for students in the 7th and 8th grades. Here the students begin enjoying group discussions of their weekly work and learn to become more independent in their study. They study logic and debate skills to help them in these discussions. Then students move into the 9th through 12th grade levels, Challenge I-IV. This is the rhetoric level of instruction, where the student shifts from being led in discussions to leading them. The community that has been growing in the previous levels is most important at this level. The Challenge levels meet concurrently with the Foundations and Essential programs during the weekly meeting.

Classical Conversations' curriculum is available to parents online and through a printed catalogue. The Foundations curriculum cycles through three historical periods over a three-year span: ancient through modern world history in Year 1, then pre-Reformation to modern world history in Year 2, and finally a year in American history. Having the students rotate through this cycle twice in the six-year program allows for the growing mind to revisit old material and add new things to it. This history is taught through the use of Classical Conversations' own Memory flash cards. Older reading students also use Susan Wise Bauer's narrative history series from Peace Hill Press. The study has a Geography component using Classical Conversations' resources as well. Their mathematics program follows the Saxon Math series. Classical Conversations offers their own hand-writing resources.

In the Essentials curriculum, Saxon is continued in math, and the program in history moves through the three-year cycle for a second time. Writing is taught using Andrew Pudewa's Institute for Excellence in Writing materials. Many of the reading materials are from primary sources. This means parents have fewer text resources to purchase, and the student begins growing a library of primary sources for himself.

In the Challenge programs, a great number of resources are offered in the catalogue. Math continues with Saxon. Latin is taken up using the Henle program. The composition program moves from Institute for Excellence in Writing material into the Lost Tools of Writing program from the CiRCE Institute. The literature selections continue to grow. Formal logic is studied first using material from Canon Press and moves to Martin Cothran's series from Memoria Press. Science is more formally entered into through the *Exploring Creation* series by J. Wile. A Curriculum Guide is available for each grade level that helps guide the parents through the year's work and the curriculum.

Classical Conversations has experienced rapid growth in its brief history. There were 50 local communities in 2006, 200 in 2008, 700 in 2010, and 1,400 communities by 2012. By the 2012-13 school year, they were serving 50,000 students at an international scope.[20] The organization and Dr. Bortins continue to refine, add to, and market their resources, online helps, and tutor development. It appears that CC will be one of the largest organizations in classical home-centered education for some time to come.

Resources

One of the obvious features of classical homeschool learning is the plethora of resources online and in print. A dizzying array of ideas, curricula, methodology help, and programs can be found with a simple Google search. The following section closes this chapter with a survey of the notable resources (by category) that a homeschool family can avail itself of in the classical education spectrum.

Online courses

Memoria - http://www.memoriapress.com/onlineschool
Circe - http://www.circeinstitute.org/online-academy
Veritas - http://resource2.veritaspress.com/Resources/Scholars_
Online/Scholars_Online_Main.html
Schola tutorials - http://www.scholatutorials.org/
Angelicum Academy (Dr. James Taylor) - http://angelicum.net/
great-books-program/

Conferences

Circe - www.circeinstitute.org
Great Homeschool Conventions - http://www.greathomeschool
conventions.com/classical-education-model

Curricula

Memoria - www.memoriapress.com
Veritas - www.veritaspress.com
Logos - http://www.logospressonline.com/
Susan Wise Bauer - http://www.welltrainedmind.com/
Mother of Divine Grace School - http://www.motherofdivine
grace.org/
Our Lady of Victory School - http://www.olvs.org/index.asp?

IX

Higher Education

Many who pursue a classical K-12 education wonder what should follow once their child graduates from high school. Are there any "classical colleges" out there? A "classical" college experience pursues the four elements of classical education: logocentric, humane, Western, and working from a classical curriculum. Unfortunately, elementary and secondary schools seem far ahead of colleges and universities in rediscovering the liberal arts. Despite the many institutions that identify themselves as "liberal arts colleges," most seem to be distancing themselves from any historic understanding of that title, rather than recovering it.

No modern American universities are organized around the "three sciences" (the natural, the moral, and the theological) and instead of championing the humanities, many are cutting the humane letters in favor of specialized and science-oriented degrees. Anti-Western stances characterize university classrooms, along with the denial of unifying or universal ideas—which was the original understanding behind "university." So while most institutions of higher education still profess a commitment to "liberal education," they have abandoned its meaning.

Much of what drives the curricula of modern colleges is the desire to ensure that graduates receive a good salary, not the desire to have a school that produces good students. Parents commonly voice the fear that their child will fail to hop on the merry-go-round of success that supposedly starts with entrance to a "good college," continues to graduation with a "good degree," and finally the landing of a "good job." Parents' worries lead to demands for "practical education." Such anxiety ignores the fact that that only about 20 percent of domestic jobs require a college education,[1] and only 30 percent of workers have a bachelors degree or higher.[2] Yet many parents want "practical" degrees, colleges comply, and so the nation moves consistently away from true liberal arts education. In the long run, this effort is counterproductive, even on the limited issue of practicality, as we shall see in this chapter.

The Rise and Fall of the Liberal Arts College

The pretense to offering a liberal education in most colleges today is generally satisfied when students select from a menu of courses said to compose a "core curriculum" or a package of "general education requirements." But there is more to a liberal arts education than that. The curriculum, including "liberal arts" requirements, has been shattered into unrelated fragments: intellectual disciplines have been narrowed to arcane specialties; and students, free to choose their courses—even to choose their requirements—graduate without any kind of coherent general education.

Often, the demise of the liberal arts is said to result from their having no practical value. "You can't get a job with a degree in the humanities,"[3] runs the argument. But many stories refute that logic. A recent article showed how several classically educated students pursued great jobs after college by using the abilities gained through their liberal arts education.[4] Their broad base of knowledge and ability to learn anything well places them high on the list of possible candidates for most jobs. And this means there are signs of hope and change.

The liberal arts offer a framework for a comprehensive education, which, far from imposing a straitjacket on the inquiring mind, has always stimulated new ideas and fresh insights.

Educational historian Bruce Kimball argues that the historic practice of the liberal arts has seesawed between logic and rhetoric.[5] A quick survey of higher educational history shows that the Greek version of the liberal arts, inspired by Socrates' attacks on the Sophists, championed logic. The Roman version, focusing on civic responsibilities, emphasized rhetoric. Medieval scholastics centered the curriculum around logic in order to know the truths of God, while Renaissance humanists favored rhetoric to exalt the excellences of man. The Enlightenment's logic-based neoclassicism swung the pendulum again, before it in turn gave way to the rhetorical aestheticism of Romantic classicists.

These shifts in emphasis suggest how a classical education can be adapted to the ethos of an age. Nonetheless, strictly speaking, a liberal arts education ought to develop both logic *and* rhetoric, truth *and* citizenship, the intellect *and* the emotions, the sciences *and* the arts. An education that is truly liberal must develop all distinctively human capacities and place them in relationship with each other. Few "Renaissance" men or women can completely balance or synthesize thought and feeling, rationality and creativity, but a liberal education strives for this kind of comprehensiveness and integration.

Educating Renaissance men and women today is particularly difficult in light of what poet T. S. Eliot called "the dissociation of sensibility."[6] Eliot observed that thought and feeling have been in conflict since the eighteenth century. Emotions were scorned during the "Age of Reason," while feelings and experience were exalted over reason and objectivity during the Romantic era that followed. The split widened in the twentieth century: artists withdrew into their own subjective feelings with little reference to objective reality, while social theorists attempted to replicate "hard" science by rigorously excluding "value judgments" from their inquiries.

It was not always this way. Eliot found no division between thought and feeling in Dante, Shakespeare, or Donne. In their poetry it is evident they "feel their thoughts." They could think about their emotions, and respond emotionally to their ideas. Their Christian worldview affirmed both the objective and subjective realms, and their liberal arts education helped them nourish this kind of "unified sensibility."

The Enlightenment, however, separated "values" from "facts." At that time, in higher education, the arts began to be divided from the sciences to the detriment of both spheres. In the late nineteenth century, American higher education split into two separate tracks: the liberal arts college (concentrating on the humanities) and the research university (concentrating on the sciences). During the early nineteenth century, most European and American universities were still citadels of classical liberal arts education. A student at Oxford or Harvard would still study Latin and Greek, read classical literature and philosophy, and attend lectures in history, mathematics, and theology without concentrating on one discipline or declaring a major field of study. The basic, liberal university education was taken as a prerequisite for entry into all professions.

Most English universities in the Victorian era were in line with the ideals set forth by John Henry Cardinal Newman in his influential book, *The Idea of a University*. Newman differentiated "useful" knowledge (that which is a means to achieve some other good) from "liberal" knowledge (that which is pursued for its own sake, because it is good in itself). One wants to know, for example, how to build a machine that weaves cloth in order to produce useful goods and make money, but to know the structure of the universe or the beauty of a work of art is worthwhile in itself. Newman argued that the pursuit of truth for its own sake was the purpose of the university, although he admitted that the development of intellect and character also had practical professional consequences.

Although the distinction between a useful and a liberal education is eminently classical, it may be that Newman's idea of the university already exhibits the dissociation of sensibility that Eliot lamented. Surely the explosion of science and technology during the nineteenth century was inadequately represented in the university curriculum. This lack of balance helped the liberal arts became synonymous with the "humanities," and given the trends in art and literature through the nineteenth and twentieth centuries, those subjects became more and more subjective and hence "impractical" and "irrelevant."

By the first decades of the twentieth century, most ostensibly "liberal arts" colleges had adopted the German university model. Almost all American colleges now featured subject majors for students, faculty specialization, and "practical" training.

Despite the victory of the research university, the twentieth century also saw a major rediscovery of the liberal arts, which altered even some research universities. Apologists for the liberal arts, such as University of Chicago president Robert Maynard Hutchins, made their case and actually persuaded the academic establishment to change its approach. What emerged was a new model for higher education: Students would pursue a liberal education in their first two years by means of a core curriculum, followed by specialized study in the last two years of their undergraduate career. After the student upheavals of the 1960s and 1970s, however, the core curriculum in much of higher education was dismantled, along with the ideal of liberal arts education.

"Cultural diversity" is now used as an argument against classical education, but in the early twentieth century cultural diversity sparked an emphasis on the liberal arts. In the years after World War I, students of various backgrounds began to enter America's universities, particularly immigrants and their children. Unable to assume a common fund of cultural knowledge, faculties did not encourage a proliferation of multi-cultural studies. Instead, educators reflected on what should be central and essential to students of all backgrounds.

At Columbia University in New York City, where immigrant collegians were especially numerous, faculty member John Erskine developed a

"Great Books" course, which the university soon expanded into an intensive, integrated core curriculum centered on the study of the key texts of Western civilization.[7]

Robert Maynard Hutchins was one product of Columbia's approach to education. In the 1930s he became president of the University of Chicago and began to reshape that institution around the principles of liberal education. The "Great Books" became central, Chicago became a center of neo-Aristotelianism, and the University has been a haven for such teacher-scholars in the classical tradition ever since, attested by the presence of Mortimer Adler, Richard Weaver (author of *Ideas Have Consequences*), and Allan Bloom (author of *The Closing of the American Mind*).

By the 1950s, almost all institutions of higher education, from the Ivy League to state land-grant colleges, had adopted the undergraduate pattern of two years of general education, organized around a core curriculum, followed by two years study directed toward a specialized major and minor. American universities became known as the best in the world during the Cold War years. But the student upheaval of the 1960s disrupted higher education, and it veered in a new direction.

Because the youth counter-culture of that era demanded "relevance," contemporary issues were deemed more important than an understanding of the past; practical knowledge was valued more than knowledge for its own sake; and social activism was put on a par with scholarly study. As former student revolutionaries earned graduate degrees, they began to join the faculties they once denounced. They politicized traditional academic disciplines and further undermined higher education's commitment to the liberal arts. The new radicalism treats the canon of "Great Books" as an arbitrary list of white male authors whose works impose a Western ideology on the powerless.

The current intellectual climate is thus intrinsically hostile to classical thought, and it is little wonder that the liberal arts are casualties. The problem with this hyper-skepticism of our civilization's past is that it undermines all knowledge and education itself. Postmodernism, which denies all hierarchies of value, "deconstructs" itself along with every other meaning system. If there is no truth, who needs college? If all meanings and beliefs are merely individual assertions, subjective impressions, or culturally determined expressions of power, then there is little reason to learn about them. A university teaching such things becomes its own victim.

A 1993 study by the National Association of Scholars (NAS) documents what it terms "the dissolution of general education." The NAS project analyzed the catalogues and program requirements from 1914-1993 of the 50 top colleges and universities as named by *U.S. News and World Report*, finding that as of 1993 only 36 percent of these institutions required English composition, 14 percent had literature requirements, 10 percent required philosophy, and a mere 12 percent had a specific history require-ment.[8] The sciences were equally affected: only 34 percent of the same 50 schools had science requirements. Mathematics requirements had dwindled from 82 percent in 1914, to 36 percent by 1939, and 12 percent in 1993.[9] The NAS study also showed that the system of organizing liberal arts knowl-edge into sequences of lower division survey courses that are prerequisites for more specialized upper division courses has virtually disappeared.[10]

Models of the New Liberal Arts

The Liberal Arts need to be redefined in our day. They have tradi-tionally been the arts necessary for the pursuing of truth, for learning, and for becoming truly free. These arts train people to think well, to speak, listen, write, and read well; in short, to do all the things necessary to the pursuit of truth. Everyone seems to agree that college students should grad-uate knowing how to do these things but are unsure how to bring it about.

State agencies and accrediting bodies are now demanding that colleges find ways to measure how much their students learn; but contemporary thought has made such judgments nonsensical. Assessment programs, however well-intentioned, are often clumsy attempts to quantify the unquantifiable that treat numbers as the only type of objective knowledge. When accrediting agencies assess colleges they compound existing problems by too often using race and gender diversity requirements and other politically correct benchmarks. And yet, efforts to measure academic quality are a tacit acknowledgment that objective standards exist, as classical educational philosophy insists. The assessment movement is a sign that the public is starting to see what happens when postmodernism takes over the classroom, and this change may help direct higher education back to the liberal arts. It appears that all serious attempts to identify the problems of higher education and to work for reform are groping towards the liberal arts, its absence being felt across the board. The time seems to be right for yet another rebirth of classical education.

Of course, a number of colleges have been keeping the classical liberal arts alive in a number of innovative ways. Some schools study the Great

Books; others incorporate a rigorously systematic core curriculum into their specialized programs; some cultivate a classical approach to education in their institutional philosophies.

The Great Books

A "Great Books" approach has students attain a liberal arts education by studying key texts of the world's intellectual heritage. The purpose of a Great Books curriculum is to form the intellect and enable the student to discern that which is true and good. This requires an understanding of the clash of ideas, a confrontation with mistakes, and an appreciation of the differing worldviews that underlie contemporary assumptions. Students participate in what Robert Maynard Hutchins called the "Great Conversation" of Western thought, and through their studies they learn to sift ideas and reach their own conclusions. A Great Books curriculum promotes genuine intellectual diversity and the student's freedom of belief, in stark contrast to the intellectual climate in most postmodernist universities, which prizes the diversity of race and gender while remaining intolerant to diverse ideas.

The pioneering institution devoted to liberal education through study of the Great Books is St. John's College.[11] Founded in 1696, it is the third oldest college in America and has campuses in Annapolis, Maryland, and Santa Fe, New Mexico. As in the classical universities of old, there are no majors and no electives; all students take the same classes. All St. John's classes use a Socratic dialectic of questions and discussion conducted by tutors who ask penetrating questions about the readings; they call upon the students and urge them to articulate and defend their ideas. With a few exceptions, St. John's has no official testing periods or graded examinations. Instead, students write essays on their reading and are evaluated face to face by panels of tutors. The pace is intense: students read an average of 80 pages per day for each class. Nearly one-third of entering students fail to graduate, but those who do are snapped up by professional schools and major corporations even though they have no declared major.

St. John's offers a secular education—though it respects religion and takes it seriously—while Thomas Aquinas College in Santa Paula, California, is unapologetically Catholic. It focuses on the Catholic intellectual tradition and is committed to the medieval tradition embodied in the Seven Liberal Arts. Other small Catholic colleges offering a great books program include Thomas More College (New Hampshire), Ave Maria University

(Florida), The College of Saint Mary Magdalen (New Hampshire), College of St. Catherine (Minnesota), and the Erasmus Institute (Massachussetts). Some Protestant counterparts would include New St. Andrews College (Idaho), Gutenburg College (Oregon), Baylor University (Texas), and Faulkner University (Alabama).

Core Curricula

Lacking a Great Books curriculum, colleges have to organize their liberal arts core course requirements carefully. Some do this well. Baylor University in Waco, Texas, for example, has an optional core in which students take courses redolent of the trivium: "Thinking and Writing" and "Thinking, Writing, and Research." Using literature to integrate studies in history, psychology, and aesthetics, Baylor offers students courses in "Introduction to Literature," "English Literature Before Burns," and the like.

Another Baptist school offering a core curriculum approach is the Houston Baptist University Honors College (Texas), which is currently in the midst of an overhaul of their program that will result in their offering one of the finest core curricula in the nation. Also worth mentioning are the core programs at Pepperdine University (California), Gustavus Adolphus College (Minnesota), Asbury College (Kentucky), Calvin College (Michigan), Union College (New York), and Whitman College (Washington). Catholic colleges in this tradition would include Providence College (Rhode Island) and St. Mary's College (Maryland).

In our own age most institutions of higher education have no institutional philosophy. Each department fiercely defends its scholarly standards to the administration while internally battling over those same standards. Faculty members pursue their own intellectual and political agendas. The best students try to learn, while others maneuver for grades and recommendations. Higher education is intellectually fragmented and resistant to authority, and its claims to public respect—and to public and private support—are undercut by the relativism and political preoccupations of the prevailing cult of postmodernism.

Some schools, however, resist these trends and have a small but noticeable effect on the academy. They give jobs to scholars and teachers who might otherwise be shut out of a hostile academic job market. They help support scholarship that refutes postmodernist claims. And by offering real alternatives, they conserve much that is under attack in contemporary education theory and practice.

Two of the most heroic of these schools are Grove City College in Grove City, Pennsylvania, and Hillsdale College in Hillsdale, Michigan. Both schools resist all government encroachment into their affairs. To maintain their independence, they have their own student aid programs and forswear all federal money, including the G.I. Bill, Pell grants, and government-insured student loans. While welcoming minorities, they have fought government racial-preference policies.

In a devastating critique of contemporary higher education, *The Fall of the Ivory Tower: Government Funding, Corruption, and the Bankrupting of American Higher Education*, former Hillsdale president George Roche surveyed the academy's ills: the emphasis on research at the expense of good teaching; stifling government regulations; skyrocketing costs and financial waste; and left-wing enforcement of politically correct dogma. He contended that these problems are consequences of federal grant money that flows to the nation's colleges and universities.[12] He credits Hillsdale's principled refusal to accept federal funds for its academic climate, which stands in marked contrast to most other schools.

Hillsdale's strong liberal arts curriculum includes study of the great books, extensive general education requirements, and—unique to Hillsdale—seminars built on campus lectures delivered by the nation's foremost conservative thinkers. Published in Hillsdale's *Imprimis* series, the lectures are widely disseminated and enable the college to speak to a national audience.[13] Hillsdale is also an incubator for alternative ideas and policies to the academic mainstream. Its department of education has established an alternative model for teacher-training programs. The department has recruited a new generation of scholars who understand classical learning and who show teachers-to-be how to teach substance as well as process, academic mastery as well as socialization skills. The department has established a model school, Hillsdale Academy, as a laboratory for faculty, training ground for student teachers, and alternative to local public schools (see chapter 4).

Grove City College also has a comprehensive liberal arts core and high academic standards, and has remained free from the taint of federal funding. Grove City's mission is beyond politics. In the words of its academic vice president, "We are rejecting what I call political, ideological, or philosophical agendas that go against objective truth as the goal of liberal learning."[14]

Contrary to the claims and expectations of many secular thinkers, colleges rooted in religious faith are among the most committed to the liberal arts. These schools accept a ground of transcendent meaning as the basis for the knowledge of truth, goodness, and beauty.

The medieval university established the liberal arts heritage for Catholic colleges. Besides those already mentioned, both the University of Dallas (Texas), and St. Vincent University (Pennsylvania) have remained dedicated to that heritage.

Homeschooling also moved into higher education in the fall of 2000 when Patrick Henry College opened its doors to students of the home-schooling revolution. This Virginia college is specifically designed for the benefit of homeschooled students. It offers a general education core based on the classical liberal arts in a community ordered around the promotion of virtue.

Professional Organizations

But despite the many successful classical alternatives to the current education establishment, the grip that relativists, post-Marxists, and nihilists have on educational theory and practice should not be underestimated. Their presence in professional organizations and accrediting agencies will influence the next generation of teachers and scholars, who in turn will shape many citizens and leaders in the arts, law, politics, and the media, with vast cultural repercussions. Before a renaissance of classical education can occur, false ideas must be refuted. This can be done best by those with the standing to challenge the intellectual establishment from within.

Professors' reputations, promotions, and salaries depend on their peers' good opinion. Campus colleagues can testify to a professor's character, teaching ability, and community service, but in the academic world, scholarly reputations are made by one's national and even international peers. Faculty scattered across the country depend on professional organizations to introduce them to colleagues in their scholarly discipline. Ordinarily, liberal arts scholars should welcome professional groups because they help maintain high standards and exercise critical judgment. While many liberal arts organizations have been commandeered by radical postmodernists who have redefined scholarly excellence according to their own standards, some organizations have arisen to stem the tide.

The National Association of Scholars (NAS) in Princeton is a network of scholars that has attracted some of the nation's most distinguished faculty in the sciences and humanities. The organization is dedicated to ideals that at one time would have been considered inarguable within the academy: reason, the pursuit of objective truth, academic freedom, and the Western heritage of intellectual inquiry. Today, however, the typical NAS member is confronted by extremely vocal and active campus colleagues who reject those ideals and attempts to overthrow their defenders. Fortunately, increasing numbers of scholars are resisting these opponents to the liberal arts.

The NAS challenges college administrations that invoke politically correct ideologies to deny academic freedom for faculty. It mobilizes opposition to destructive academic policies, and through its journal, *Academic Questions*, it subjects postmodernist scholarship to withering criticism. It defends Western civilization courses and programs against multi-culturalist attacks, has filed suit against speech codes that restrict expression of politically incorrect ideas, and documents the erosion of higher education.

The general public and graduates of once-distinguished institutions have little idea about what is taught—and what is not taught—on most college campuses today. Simply informing people about the state of academia can be an important catalyst for reform. The American Council of Trustees and Alumni (ACTA) is an organization that seeks to organize alumni concerned about the fate of schools they once attended. Just as proponents of a more classical education have organized like-minded members of the faculty and formed their own professional organizations, so also have they established a way to voice the discontent of alumni across the country. ACTA urges alumni, especially alumni donors and trustees of governing boards, to take a second look at their alma mater and ask: How are their financial gifts used? What are administrators doing with their authority? Such attention can only help the cause of classical reform.

Accrediting bodies wield enormous power in the world of higher education: without accreditation, students at an institution will lose access to financial aid, and the institution itself will be hard-pressed to obtain governmental and private funds. Accrediting agencies have helped improve American higher education by insisting on assessments of institutional performance, but in recent years, some have used the assessment process to impose gender, race, and ethnic "diversity" requirements on course curricula, student admissions, and faculty hiring and promotion. Schools reluctant to subordinate their intellectual standards to the new requirements of race and gender have come under pressure from accrediting committees.[15]

One regional accrediting agency for California took on Thomas Aquinas College, a Catholic school wholly devoted to the seven liberal arts and to the Catholic Church's intellectual heritage. Though the college has unusually high academic standards, the agency complained that it lacked diversity, insisting that the college's list of Great Books should include more works by women and minorities, and even complaining that the student body and faculty lacked diversity. Aquinas' president, Dr. Thomas Dillon, resisted these mandates, defying the accrediting agency and resolving to take it to court. The accrediting agency backed down.

To deal with such incidences, an alternative accrediting agency has been organized. The American Academy for Liberal Education (AALE) will not accredit a school unless its curriculum has a foundation in the liberal arts. AALE also accredits K-12 schools.[16] But although the creation of an accrediting agency sympathetic to the liberal arts is wise, it cannot independently establish and maintain institutions like Thomas Aquinas College. The restoration of classical education in higher education ultimately depends on the wisdom and courage of college administrators, trustees, and faculty who will stand for its principles—and on a similar wisdom among parents who recognize that an exclusive focus on "practicality" may not even serve that goal, much less the goal of forming their children for lives of wisdom and virtue.

X

Myths and Realities of Classical Education

In recent years, the classical education renewal has garnered increased attention. From local newspapers to CNN and the *New York Times*, the media have reported on the growth of classical schooling. Across the nation, classical schools of various stripes are being established: religious, non-religious, grammar schools, high schools, university model schools, public charter schools, and homeschooling cooperatives. While they take different forms, these schools' commitment to classical education is marked by certain common elements.

What Classical Schools Do

The classical school is committed to a liberal, or general, curriculum. It is "general" in that its territory is all human knowledge, from the arts to the sciences, history to mathematics. The curriculum does not claim a narrow field of specialization or market niche for itself. Nor does it permit students to evade issues they cannot understand or ways of thinking they cannot handle. Instead, it helps them confront sources of misunderstanding and develop their intellectual powers. The curriculum is "liberal" in that it is rooted in the seven liberal arts: grammar, logic, rhetoric, arithmetic, geometry, astronomy, and music. From the Latin *liber*, meaning "free," the liberal arts aim at freeing students for self-government and nurturing the growth of wisdom and virtue in them.

The classical school explicitly or implicitly recognizes and applies the principles of the trivium (grammar, logic, rhetoric), keyed to the stages of the student's intellectual development and to the universal process of learning. It provides training in language and logic, and in writing and speech. The curriculum also understands the principles of the quadrivium (arithmetic, geometry, astronomy, and music) and insists that a good education encompasses abstract thought, aesthetic appreciation, empirical

113

inquiry, and spatial relation. It applies these "arts" of learning to the "sciences" of the natural world, and the social world, and the realm of religious faith and meaning.

Classical schools integrate all elements of the curriculum, and learning is unified and cumulative. Students are taught to recognize how areas of knowledge relate to one another, and how basic knowledge learned in earliest childhood is the foundation for more complex ways of knowing.

Classical schools do not denigrate or ignore the past; neither are they nostalgic for it. Acknowledging the continuum of history, classical schools build on the great ideas, discoveries, and expressions of those who have gone before. They borrow pedagogical forms, such as the trivium, and often require or encourage study of Greek and Latin. The great ideas of the past are a starting point—not the last word—for the "great conversation" into which classical education escorts students. Classical educator David Hicks endorses a poised and balanced understanding of this when he insists that, "The true knowledge of *paideia* requires a discerning appreciation for the past, unprejudiced by an assumption of progress or regress."

Classical schools cultivate a student's interest in first principles and ultimate purposes. They are not afraid to delve deeply into philosophy and religion, but encourage questions and answers about knowledge, faith, and meaning. Teachers in classical schools provoke students to ask about the purpose of education and are not satisfied with money and career as answers.

Classical schools inculcate wisdom and virtue. Children yearn to become adults, and a classical education prepares them for adult responsibilities: for working and earning a living, raising a family, the privileges and duties of citizenship and friendship, and for courage in the face of solitude, illness, and death. Career counseling and technical training will count for little if our schools are unable to nurture the moral character of their students. Ironically, the desire for a well-paying job—which many parents and children consider education's only purpose—has failed to motivate many students to study hard and learn well.

Classical schools educate for citizenship. Without an education in wisdom and virtue, citizens give way to alienation, apathy, and intemperance and this leads to family and neighborhood disintegration, crime, and political corruption. Modernism and postmodernism can scarcely speak to such concerns with a straight face.

Finally, classical schools are communities of learning. Because teachers and students share an idealistic and even visionary aim, their schools are humane, disciplined, and stimulating. Classical education is deeply personal: teachers are coaches, midwives, and mentors of their students. Their classes are not organized around lectures and multiple choice tests; they are Socratic dialogues that provoke clear thinking and fresh insights. Classical schools make demands on students, but they also inspire them.

Misconceptions about Classical Education

Classical education is not elitist. True, the wealthy are more likely to send their children to private schools that appreciate the importance of the liberal arts, but this argues for making such schools more, not less, accessible to all.

Classical education is not traditionalist or reactionary. It hails achievements, not eras, and only honors traditions that represent inherently worthy ideas and practices. Classical education values the testimony of personal experience, but does not glorify it.

Some equate classical education with the humanities, and contrast it to mathematics and science. But this confuses the classical understanding of the "humanities" with what it has come to mean, namely, a near-exclusive focus on literature and the arts. Cicero, who coined the term, meant an education fit for a Roman, comprising all that man could achieve, including arithmetic, geometry, music, the arts, and the trivium of grammar, logic, and rhetoric. Properly understood, a classical education values *all* branches of learning and seeks to prevent the unbalanced concentration of studies that too often produces the "artsy" student or the "science nerd."

Some critics believe classical education is authoritarian and stifles creativity. They imagine a teacher rapping the knuckles of the student who has not formed his letters correctly or forcing children to memorize trivial facts and repeat boring drills. These are myths. Yes, the work load is great, discipline is strict, and there is plenty of drill, especially in grammar school. But the purpose of it all is to make possible the adult's creative and independent thought (*libera*).

Others believe classical education's commitment to the search for truth disguises a mentality of dogmatic certainty. Nothing could be more false. Unlike postmodernism, which is dogmatically certain that all knowledge is relativist, classical education believes in the possibility of objective knowledge and truth. The mind that knows that it does not know everything—

that possesses the humility of Socrates—still longs to know the truth. This is not "dogmatism" in the pejorative sense of indoctrination and narrow-mindedness. The method of classical learning is dialectic, a process of questioning. Dialectic encourages openness to truth in all its complexity and mystery; it does not lead to an unyielding skepticism or any other kind of closed dogmatism. Classical education nourishes wonder; it provokes the curiosity and inquisitiveness that leads to scientific discovery, and it inclines the mind to ultimate questions of religious faith.

Growing Pains

Classical education is growing in popularity and, like any movement, is experiencing growing pains. But many of the obstacles that classical schools face can be reduced to one overarching problem: classical education is hard and American culture tends to turn away from hard things, especially for the young. In general, Americans are anxious to hear that everything is all right for their children. It's easy to persuade them that their schools are fine, that even though under-funded urban schools may have problems, "our" local schools do not.

But what makes a good school? Are its graduates wiser for having attended it? Americans today uncritically accept the empirical mindset; we are easily persuaded by statistics. But is a student really better prepared for the moral and academic challenges of college if he has higher scores on a statistics-based test? Can those scores make up for a taste that is vulgar and excessive, for indolence and cynicism?

Proud of our pragmatism and casual habits, Americans are not supposed to be a philosophical people. We are embarrassed to speak of transcendental concerns like wisdom and virtue, or truth, goodness, and beauty. But it is precisely because we are obsessed with the particulars on the periphery instead of the great ideas in the center that classical education is a moral necessity for our age.

Because classical schools in America minister within such a culture, they face growing pains within each of the "five perspectives" of school life: *pedagogy, curriculum, assessment, governance,* and *community.* While these five perspectives ought to be viewed as threads in a tapestry, rather than as separate elements, it may help to view the needs of each perspective individually.

Pedagogy

Classical education is difficult for the teachers in classical schools. They have inadequate curricular resources to master the skills of teaching—though these are rapidly improving—and they are raising families on an insufficient salary. Teachers in classical schools make enormous sacrifices, often for little reward. Indeed, if teachers in public schools can claim to be underpaid, then most teachers in classical schools are living in abject poverty.

Classical schools also must train or re-train their teachers. Those who have graduated from state certification programs are not trained for the classical school. Many have a cynical attitude toward knowledge and are obsessed with technique. Consequently, some classical schools prefer not to hire teachers who are certified because they have so much to "unlearn" from their college training. But this often means schools hire teachers with little training in classroom management or teaching methodology. While many classical schools do take teacher training seriously, classical teachers often must learn their materials and craft on the fly.

As a result of these difficulties, teachers often struggle with learning to teach from a state of rest, rather than out of anxiety, or a desire to "get through" the material. Teachers must add the discipline of contemplation—in themselves and their students—particularly through the practice of mimetic and Socratic teaching. Mimetic instruction guides students to meditate on models or types in order to present ideas in concrete form so students can understand an idea or truth and then apply it. Socratic instruction, which is more than simply "asking questions," guides students to meditate on ideas so they can use deduction to clarify and apply an idea. These "two modes" of teaching are focused on the cultivation of understanding and the perception of truth. More directly, classical schools must train and encourage teachers to teach classically.

Curriculum

Classical schools must also develop a more robust understanding of curriculum, moving beyond the initially helpful, but very limiting, view that the trivium is the entirety of classical education. A classical curriculum must be structured upon the *seven* liberal arts, not simply grammar, logic, and rhetoric. Schools must grow to understand and apply the quadrivium, the other four liberal arts of arithmetic, geometry, astronomy, and music.

Several particular needs could be addressed here. The curriculum must be seen as integrated, not divided or compartmentalized neatly into "subjects." Latin and Greek, the languages upon which Western civilization was established, should be taught, and taught for mastery, not merely as a means of boosting standardized test scores. Math and science must be taught mimetically, and classical schools must rid themselves of the erroneous notion that "classical" means "humanities only."

Assessment

Perhaps more than any other area, the practice of assessment presents problems for classical schools. Knowing that the purpose of education is to nurture the soul, classical schools struggle with the American obsession over grades, quantifiable results, and pinpoint measurement of students down to the thousandth decimal place. Such anxieties tempt classical school parents, students, board members, and even many administrators and teachers to change their "classical tune" when it comes to assessment.

Modern methods of assessment are abstract, not personal, and are based upon an industrialized form of schooling, all characteristics that run contrary to classical education. How does one measure the nurturing of the soul via Scantron bubbles? What number value can be placed upon a student's growth in wisdom and virtue?

Classical schools must learn to assess students in a manner consistent with the mimetic and Socratic instruction they receive. Assessment should be personal and normative, not abstract and relative. The standard should be whether a student has mastered the art or science, not whether they used the right tricks to temporarily memorize information and regurgitate it on the test. Under modern assessment methods, students can maintain the appearance of knowledge and intelligence without any of the substance. Modern assessment is, therefore, horribly impractical.

It is important to recognize that the discussion of assessment is just beginning, which means classical schools have an exciting opportunity to experiment with better ways of assessing students. Given how deeply entrenched most schools are in grading scales and numbers, a change in mindset must occur throughout the school community: board members, headmasters, teachers, and parents. If the nature of assessment is misunderstood by those leading the school, then the likelihood of change to more beneficial assessments remains small.

Classical schools should consider experimenting with potential assessment methods in one class and then evaluating the result. Teachers can help matters by distinguishing between the types of learning occurring in their classes—knowledge, skills, and understanding—and assessing appropriately. For example, students wrestling with the question, "Should the conspirators have assassinated Julius Caesar?" would not be profitably assessed by a multiple choice test. Headmasters can help by clarifying the real goals of teaching—the cultivation of wisdom and virtue, growth in judgment and understanding of truth—and continuing the discussion of assessment with their faculty.

Governance

School boards also find classical education a difficult proposition. Frequently, classical school supporters have little experience and knowledge about how the schools work. Rare is the school board organized by classical scholars or men and women who have been classically educated. Some boards make the mistake of simplifying classical education to a manageable formula like Dorothy Sayers' trivium, and minimizing the importance of classical languages and texts, or mathematics.

Some boards lack governing experience while others rely on experience from the business world, failing to recognize that a school is a fundamentally different organism. Failing to understand the nature of a school leads to tremendous trouble. A school's success cannot be measured by profits, but must grow from a shared vision. Lacking one, schools can easily become distracted from their mission. The role of the board must be to prevent such distractions; it must continually clarify and deepen the school's understanding of the classical vision.

The board needs to explain and defend the vision to parents. Some parents will want to become more involved in the school, yet if too many are well-meaning but uninformed they may undercut the classical vision. Still, no school can succeed without the support of parents. School boards have to struggle to manage this dilemma while also providing resources for the school and its teachers.

Of course, these problems are not insoluble. Americans are more concerned with big ideas than our media-driven self-image would suggest. Classical school boards, teachers, and parents are usually devoted to their work, will stay the course, and will resist those who, following Locke, regard the soul as a "needless hypothesis." They will return education to its proper function of feeding the soul with its rightful food: truth, goodness, and beauty.

The most decisive factor, however, must be clear visionary leadership, and it should be embodied in the person who heads the school. The primary duty of the board is to find this leader and to empower him. The three most foolish things a board can do are (1) fail to hire such a person; (2) hire someone the board cannot trust with this burden, and (3) undercut him once he is appointed.

The visionary leader will carry the classical vision in his soul. He will communicate and represent it to parents, winning their confidence. He will stand behind teachers and equip them to carry the vision into the classroom. He will understand that he must fight the prevailing culture, and he will engage that fight with the weapons of the gentleman. The leader's personality, formed by his love of classical learning, will form the personality of the school. For in the end, classical education is personal and seeks the development of the person. This is what it means to be humane. When classical education is enshrined in the person, it takes root in the community and the family. When it is not, it fades into an unrealized dream. For this reason, the worst mistake a headmaster (or board) can make is thinking analytically rather than normatively. As David Hicks has said, "The aims of education, the teacher's methods, the books and lessons, the traditions, and the regulations of the school—all must express not just ideas, but norms, tending to make young people not only rational, but noble." Classical schools must be governed with such aims in mind.

Supporters of the classical movement must support the work of these visionary leaders. We have discussed the role of parents and school boards, but external supports, such as associations, conference organizers, consulting services, and curriculum publishers have a role as well. Visionary leaders need time to reflect, and they need people with whom to reflect. They need resources to develop their teachers and teach their families. They need curricula that avoid sentimentalism and excess, but recognize metaphor and beauty in children's literature. They need, in the end, to be allowed to be what they yearn to be: classically educated.

Community

Classical education is hard for parents. We want to feel good about the schools our children attend. The "experts" have persuaded us that form, discipline, and restraint will inhibit the self-realization of our children, so it is hard to watch a child struggle in frustration with his homework assignments. Adults in earlier ages agreed with the Lamenter when he said,

"It is good for a man to bear the yoke in his youth," but contemporary parents respond with sentimental pity because they want childhood to be easy and endless fun.

It is especially difficult for homeschooling moms who have to "take the bull by the horns." Their children will need parental help, but because most parents never learned what classical education teaches, classical education exposes what the parent hasn't learned and asks her to learn it for the child's sake.

Children have always rebelled and will always rebel against a classical education. It demands hard work from those who have yet to experience the truth of Virgil's once famous dictum, *labor omnia vincit* ("work conquers all"). Classical education also reminds children that they are not self-sufficient, that they need their wiser elders to explain the world to them, that they must learn restraint and discipline before they earn the right to expression. The difference today is not that children try to escape hard work, but that they have the sympathy of their parents and the support of a culture that actually fears children will be harmed by hard work and self-restraint. Parents must understand and fully embrace the beauty and necessity of classical education, and not only when their children are having an easy time of it.

The Future of Classical Education

We do not propose that classical education return us to the glories of Greece, the grandeur of Rome, the scholasticism of the Middle Ages, the artistry of the Renaissance, or even the moralism of Victorian England. Our times portend a new age of discovery that will require new kinds of learning.

But the past is in our present, and what we can know is contained in what we already know. We do well to avoid the fatal and arrogant conceit of jettisoning our heritage. That heritage is not solely a gift of wisdom and virtue. It also contains cautions and forewarnings. Sophistry and cynicism were characteristics of the Hellenistic world, which eventually saw its culture decline as Roman civilization rose predominant. Multiculturalism was part of everyday life in Imperial Rome, which eventually fell under the assault of barbarians. Cultural meltdown was a recurring phenomenon in the ancient world and it threatens our own time. Classical education reminds us of this bigger picture.

Classical education employs the wisdom of the past to address present needs. Older and wiser teachers instruct the young so they will not have to pursue the illusions of their predecessors or repeat their mistakes. By contrast, the "progressive" theory of education arms the young with methods of inquiry but keeps them ignorant of the truths that were once thought and said. Classical education has been midwife to centuries of cultural transformation. It has always played a paradoxical double role: preserving the past in order to usher in change and improvement.

We need a new vision of education. Many of our needs are urgent and unmet because our ideas about what education can accomplish are inadequate or false. Classical education can recover the tools of learning.

In lauding its virtues, we should not obscure the difficulties that classical education will encounter. Classical education goes against the grain of contemporary culture. It makes pampered children work hard. It forces the television generation to read. It runs counter to the anti-intellectualism prevalent among so many private and public educators. Classical school teachers will have to convince students that the good, the true, and the beautiful have more value than the glittering prizes of pop culture and the easy answers of relativism. How many parents will be like those who pulled their children from Marva Collins' school because she demanded too much? Classical schools may also face pressure from ever-growing federal interventions in education, particularly in light of the most recent and far-reaching Common Core legislation.

Additionally, many parents become blinded by fear over their child's future, and too many high school parents make test scores and college resources their main concern. Not surprisingly, students become overly stressed about college admissions as well. In turn, even teachers and head-masters can fall to the pressure of such parental demands and "marketing the school." Rather than being driven by sound, classical educational philosophy and trying to inform students and parents, they dive back into the vicious "college degree-career-money" cycle, swept away in the tide of accreditation concerns, scholarship numbers, and college acceptance lists. Such anxiety may increase as colleges, many suffering financial panic, intensify pressures on parents, students, and high schools. In attempting to boost their own enrollment, colleges may move to make college acceptance, attendance, and graduation seem even more indispensible.

And yet wherever classical education has been tried, students have learned to think broadly, deeply, and creatively. They have learned to live up to their responsibilities and to recognize the possibility of greatness within themselves.

Analyzing the classical education ideas of Thomas Aquinas, Pierre Conway and Benedict Ashley observed that the liberal arts' capacity to tap the mind's potential was not fully realized in the medieval university. Nor did the Greeks or the Renaissance masters fully recognize the richness of their education theories. "If this curriculum is not at present anywhere genuinely followed," they note, "it need not be because it is seven hundred years too late—it may simply be that it is still just a year or so too soon."[1]

Perhaps the year is now upon us.

Appendix

Organizations & Resources

The Academy at Houston Baptist University
7502 Fondren Road
Houston, TX 77074
(281) 649-3661
www.hbuacademy.com

American Classical League
Miami University
422 Wells Mill Drive
Oxford, OH 45056
(513) 529-7741
www.aclclassics.org

> *Long-time champions for the study of Latin and Greek. Makes*
> *available many resources for cultivating classical languages and culture.*

Association of Classical and Christian Schools
PO Box 9741
Moscow, ID 83843
(208) 882-6101
www.accsedu.org

> *Pioneering organization of Christian schools, organized around the*
> *Trivium. ACCS publishes curriculum guides and other materials, holds*
> *an annual conference, and offers accreditation for classical and*
> *Christian schools.*

CiRCE Institute
4190 Brownwood Lane
Concord, NC 28027
(704) 794-2227
www.circeinstitute.org

> *The CiRCE Institute is a leading provider of inspiration, information, and insight to classical educators throughout the U.S. and Canada via an annual conference, an online classical academy, in-house teacher training, Lost Tools of Writing™ Workshops and materials, consulting on board development, school leadership, and school start-up, as well as a content-laden website and blog.*

Classical Conversations
250 MacDougall Drive
P.O. Box 909
West End, NC 27376
(910) 673-0100
www.classicalconversations.com

> *Classical Conversation is a leader in "the home-centered education movement by equipping parents and students with the classical tools of learning needed to discover the order and beauty of God's creation and to inspire others to do the same."*

Classical Academic Press
2151 Market Street
Camp Hill, PA 17011
(866) 730-0711
www.classicalacademicpress.com

> *Created by Dr. Christopher Perrin, Classical Academic Press is a publisher of classical education resources and curriculum for Latin, Greek, logic, writing, and more.*

Escondido Tutorial Service
2634 Bernardo Avenue
Escondido, CA 92029
www.gbt.org

> *Offering online tutorials in the Great Books, classical Greek, science, math, and more. The classes are available to homeschoolers, other interested students, and adults.*

Great Books Honors College at Faulkner University
5345 Atlanta Highway
Montgomery, AL 36109
(334) 272-5820 or (800) 879-9816
www.faulkner.edu
www.studyliberalarts.org

Memoria Press
4603 Poplar Level Road
Louisville, KY 40213
(877) 862-1097
www.memoriapress.com

> *"Memoria Press is a family-run publishing company that produces simple and easy-to-use classical Christian education materials for home and private schools. It was founded by Cheryl Lowe in 1994 to help promote and transmit the classical heritage of the Christian West through an emphasis on the liberal arts and the great works of the Western tradition."*

National Paideia Center
29½ Page Avenue
Asheville, NC 28801
(828) 575-5592
www.paideia.org

New College Franklin
P.O. Box 1575
Franklin, TN 37065
(615) 815-8360
www.newcollegefranklin.org

New Saint Andrews College
405 South Main Street
P.O. Box 9025
Moscow, ID 83843
www.nsa.edu
(208) 882-1566

Rivendell Sanctuary
6820 Auto Club Road
Suite T
Bloomington, MN 55438
(952) 996-1451
www.rivendell.sdcc.edu

Schola Classical Tutorials
P. O. Box 546
Potlatch, ID 83855
www.scholatutorials.org

> *"Schola Classical Tutorials offers live group tutorials over the internet
> in the subjects of a classical Christian liberal arts curriculum:
> the classical languages, the great books of literature and history,
> and rhetoric."*

Society for Classical Learning
3400 Brook Road
Richmond, VA 23227
www.societyforclassicallearning.org

> *"A professional society committed to promoting the cultural benefits of the classical, Christian traditions by providing leadership and support, opportunities for the exchange of ideas, and standards of excellence for educators and schools."*

Ambleside International
P.O. Box 2976
Fredericksburg, TX. 78624
www.amblesideschools.com

Ambleside Online
www.amblesideonline.org

> *"Ambleside Online is a free homeschool curriculum that uses Charlotte Mason's classically-based principles to prepare children for a life of rich relationships with everything around them: God, humanity, and the natural world."*

Veritas Press
1805 Olde Homestead Lane
Lancaster, PA 17601
www.veritaspress.com

The Institute for Catholic Liberal Education
P.O. Box 4638
Ventura, California 93007
www.catholicliberaleducation.org

Aquinas Learning Center
P.O. Box 253
Manassas, VA 20108
www.aquinaslearning.org

Mother of Divine Grace School
407 Bryant Circle
Suite B1
Ojai, CA 93023
www.motherofdivinegrace.org

The Barney Charter School Initiative
www.hillsdale.edu/outreach/charterschools

Great Hearts Academies
3102 N. 56th St.
Suite 300
Phoenix, AZ 85018
www.greatheartsaz.org

Endnotes

Chapter I. The Lost Content of Learning

[1] John Dewey, "The Influence of Darwin on Philosophy," in *The Influence of Darwin on Philosophy and Other Essays* (New York: Henry Holt and Company, 1910), pp. 1-19.

[2] Ibid.

[3] Ibid.

[4] From a publication of the Division of Professional Development and Training, Wisconsin Education Association Council, 1994. Quoted by Charles Sykes, *Dumbing Down Our Kids: Why American Children Feel Good about Themselves but Can't Read, Write, or Add* (New York: St. Martin's Press, 1995), p. 236.

[5] Carole Edelsky et al., *Whole Language: What's the Difference?* (Portsmouth, N.H.: Heinemann, 1991).

[6] See Damon Darlin, "Back to Basics, Again," Forbes, June 17, 1996; Art Levine, "The Great Debate Revisited," *Atlantic Monthly*, December 1994; and Christina Duff, "ABCeething," *Wall Street Journal*, October 30, 1996. A study sponsored by the National Institute of Child Health and Human Development at the University of Houston has shown conclusively that phonics is the best way to teach reading.

[7] Howard Gardner, *The Disciplined Mind: Beyond Facts and Standardized Tests, The K-12 Education Program That Every Child Deserves* (New York: Penguin, 2000), p. 56.

Chapter IV. Democratic Classicism

[1] The phrases "Paideia school" and "Paideia educators" are used in this book to refer to educators and schools that realize to some appropriate degree the ideas set forth in the Paideia Group's *The Paideia Proposal* and *The Paideia Program*. "Paideia" is used to refer to the theory and practices of the radical educational reform proposed in *The Paideia Proposal* and *The Paideia Program*.

2   Interestingly, Adler himself became increasingly religious over his long life. Raised in a nonobservant Jewish family, he was drawn to ancient pagan philosophers in his teens; in his twenties, Thomas Aquinas's *Summa theologiae* attracted him, largely because of the way this medieval theologian developed Aristotle's thought. Late in life, Adler joined the Catholic Church. His friend the philosopher Ralph McInerny once heard him speak of "the transition in his own life from being intellectually convinced of the existence of God to loving the God that he knew. The philosopher's God became incarnate in Christ, and finally Adler saw that his long quest for wisdom could best be seen as a kind of *Imitatio Christi*" ("imitation of Christ"). Ralph McInerny, "Memento Mortimer," *First Things*, November 2001.

3   Mortimer Adler, *Reforming Education: The Opening of the American Mind* (New York: Collier, MacMillan, 1988), 66-67.

4   Ibid, 280.

5   *Reforming Education*, xv.

6   *Reforming Education*, 58-60.

7   *Paideia Proposal*, 3.

8   Ibid., 78.

9   *Reforming Education*, 309-310.

10 *The Paideia Proposal*, 24.

11 http://www.learnnc.org/lp/editions/paideia/6887.

12 *The Paideia Proposal*, 29.

13 *The Paideia Proposal*, 30.

14 *The Paideia Program*, 18.

15 Ibid.

16 http://www.greatbooks.org/?id=1270.

17 http://www.paideia.org/about-paideia/teaching-practices/.

18 *Teaching Critical Thinking: Using Seminars for 21st Century Literacy,* ix.

19 Ibid., x.

20 http://www.paideia.org/about-paideia/research-and-results/#teacher

21 *Paideia Program,* 3.

22 Ibid.

23 Ibid., 4.

24 Daniel Scoggin, "Classical Revolution," *GreatHearts* 1 (Fall 2008): 22.

25 Ibid.

26 *Academy Lane* [Hillsdale Academy Newsletter] (Winter, 2009): 4.

27 http://www.hillsdale.edu/academy/about/profile.asp.

28 Kenneth Calvert, headmaster of Hillsdale Academy, telephone conversation.

29 Kenneth Calvert, email communication.

30 Kenneth Calvert, telephone conversation.

31 http://www.estanciavalleyclassical.com/about.html.

32 http://www.hillsdale.edu/outreach/charterschools/new.

Chapter V. Norms and Nobility

1 David V. Hicks, *Norms and Nobility: A Treatise on Education* (1981; New York: University Press of America, 1999), p. vi.

2 Ibid., p. 69.

3 Ibid., 71.

4 Ibid., 69.

5 C.S. Lewis, *The Abolition of Man* (New York: HarperOne, 2009).

6 Hicks, *Norms and Nobility,* p. 110.

7   Interview with David Hicks (2012).

8   Hicks, *Norms and Nobility*, p. vi.

9   The Lost Tools of Writing is produced by The CiRCE Institute
    (www.circeinstitute.org).

Chapter VI. Catholic Classicism

1   "It was the request of the Catholics for state funds for their schools
    which precipitated the constitutional provisions or amendments to
    state constitutions forbidding the use of public money to aid any
    institution in which any denominational tenet or doctrine was
    taught." See William French, *America's Educational Tradition: An
    Interpretive History* (Boston: D.C. Heath and Company, 1964),
    p. 286. For the broader anti-religious effect of these "Blaine"
    amendments, see Philip Hamburger, *Separation of Church and State*
    (Cambridge: Harvard University Press, 2002).

2   John Convey, *Catholic Schools Make a Difference: Twenty-five Years
    of Research* (Washington, D.C.: National Catholic Educational
    Association, 1992), p. 35.

3   Peter Hastings, "Openness and Intellectual Challenge in Catholic
    Schools", in Terence McLaughlin, Joseph O'Keefe, and Bernadette
    O'Keeffe, *The Contemporary Catholic School: Context, Identity and
    Diversity* (London: RoutledgeFalmer, 1996), pp. 272-283.

4   *Documents of Vatican II*, "Declaration on Religious Freedom,"
    article 3.

5   Ibid., article 4.

6   Convey, p. 36.

7   National Catholic Education Association, *Annual Data Report*,
    available at ncea.org.

8   Ibid.

9   CristoReyNetwork.org.

10 National Catholic Education Association, Annual Data Report.

11 Ray Pennings et al., *Cardus Education Survey* (Hamilton, Ontario:
    Cardus, 2011), p. 13.

12 Laura Behrquist, *Designing Your Own Classical Curriculum* (San Francisco: Ignatius Press, 1998), p. 7.

13 Archbishop J. Michael Miller, "The Holy See's Teaching on Catholic Schools," catholiceducation.org/articles/education/ed0269.html.

14 Ibid., quoting the Sacred Congregation for Catholic Education, "Lay Catholics in Schools: Witnesses to Faith," http://www.vatican.va/roman_curia/congregations/ccatheduc/documents/rc_con_ccatheduc_doc_19821015_lay-catholics_en.html.

15 Miller, ibid.

16 Ibid.

17 Ibid.

18 Ibid.

19 Ibid.

20 Pope Pius XI, *Divini illius magistri* ("On Christian Education") 1929, articles 94, 95.

21 http://www.WaysideAcademy.com/about-us/approach.

22 Margaret Crotty, "Kolbe Academy … An Idea Becomes a Reality," *Immaculata magazine*, June-July 1981. Most information on Kolbe Academy in this chapter can be found on its website.

23 http://www.kolbe.org/about-us/kolbes-history/graduate-statistics.

24 Walter Burghardt, S.J., "Eloquentia Perfecta: Yesterday and Today" *AJCU Higher Education Report*, February 1998.

25 Robert Spencer, "Speak, Write, Act," http://www.kolbe.org/files/4613/9956/5482/Speak_Write_Act.pdf.

26 James M. Day, "Recognition and Responsivity: Unlearning the Pedagogy of Estrangement for a Catholic Moral Education," in McLaughlin, O'Keefe, and O'Keeffe, *The Contemporary Catholic School*, pp. 162-73.

Chapter VII. Liberating Classicism

1 From video on school's website, http://www.youtube.com/watch?feature=player_embedded&v=WskDbeu5AlQ.

2 Personal interview with Mr. Tutler, Dec. 5, 2011.

3 Personal interview with Andrew Hart, Dec. 2011.

4 See www.HopeSchool.org.

5 Personal interview with Russ Gregg, Nov. 28, 2011.

6 From the school's philosophy of education: www.HopeSchool.org.

7 See http://www.hopeschool.org/academics/curriculum.shtml.

8 From online news story, http://abclocal.go.com/wls/story?section=news/local&id=6188122.

9 Personal interview, September 5, 2013.

10 See the school website, http://www.VeritasNC.org/school-within-school.

11 Interview with program director, Allison Burdette, March 14, 2013.

12 From the school's statement of philosophy, http://www.flintacademy.com/philosophy.htm.

13 Interview with Paula Flint, August 2010.

14 Ibid.

15 Cheryl Swope, *Simply Classical: A Beautiful Education for Any Child* (Louisville, Ky.: Memoria Press, 2013), p. 17.

Chapter VIII. Classical Homeschooling

1 U.S. Department of Education, "Parent and Family Involvement in Education, from the National Household Education Surveys Program of 2012," August 2013.

2 Heather Shirley, e-mail January 13, 2012.

3 http://www.mhla.org/information/massdocuments/mglhistory.htm.

4   http://www.educationnews.org/parenting/number-of-home
    schoolers-growing-nationwide.

5   http://www.hslda.org/docs/study/ray2009/2009_Ray_Study
    FINAL.pdf.

6   Rebecca Winters, "From Home to Harvard": *Time Magazine,*
    September 3, 2000. http://content.time.com/time/magazine/
    article/0,9171,53959,00.html

7   Jessie Wise and Susan Wise Bauer, *The Well-Trained Mind: A Guide
    to Classical Education at Home* (New York: Norton, 1999), p. 47.

8   Charlotte Mason, *The Original Home Schooling Series* (6 vols.,
    Portland, Ore.: Charlotte Mason Research & Supply, 1989).

9   Susan Schaeffer Macaulay, *For the Children's Sake: Foundations of
    Education for Home and School* (Carol Stream, Ill.: Crossway,
    2009).

10 http://www.amblesideschools.com/manual/Charlotte-Mason/
    charlotte-mason-6-volume-series.

11 Anne White, "An Introduction to Charlotte Mason," available at
    https://www.amblesideonline.org/WhatIsCM.shtml.

12 Ibid.

13 Bauer and Wise, p. 38.

14 Ibid., pp. 51-54.

15 Ibid., p. 199.

16 Ibid., p. 239.

17 Ibid., p. 473.

18 Ibid., p. 47.

19 *Classical Conversations Catalogue,* 2013, p. 5.

20 Personal email from Jason Nale, area director for Eastern North
    Carolina, May 2013.

Chapter IX. Higher Education

[1] U.S. Bureau of Labor Statistics, *Monthly Labor Review*, January 2012, table 6.

[2] U.S. Census Bureau, "Bachelor's Degree Attainment Tops 30 Percent for the First Time, Census Bureau Reports," February 23, 2012.

[3] Consider the comments of radio talk show host Rush Limbaugh on this topic by reading a response to his views by the classical educator Christopher Perrin at http://insideclassicaled.com/?p=465. Perrin notes that many Americans who have succeeded in practical affairs have had classical education, from Thomas Jefferson and other Founders to today's *Fortune* 500 CEOs.

[4] Michael Reneau, "Classical and Practical?" *World magazine* September 7, 2013.

[5] See Bruce A. Kimball, *Orators and Philosophers: A History of the Idea of Liberal Education* (New York: College Entrance Examination Board, 1995).

[6] See "The Metaphysical Poets," in Frank Kermode, ed., *Selected Prose of T. S. Eliot* (New York: Harcourt, Brace, Jovanovich, 1975), pp. 59-67.

[7] See Charles Sykes and Brad Miner, *The National Review College Guide: America's Top 50 Liberal Arts Schools* (Wolgemuth & Hyatt, 1991), p. 37. For a wonderful account of how well this program is loved at Columbia, even now, read David Denby's article "Lit Hum Revisited," which can be found at www.college.columbia.edu/cct/spring13/columbia_forum.

[8] *The Dissolution of General Education: 1914-1993* (Princeton, N.J.: National Association of Scholars, 1996), pp. 22-24, 29-31. The NAS study surveys only the "top 50" institutions. Less prestigious state and church-related institutions retain more requirements and, paradoxically, may offer a better general education. Nevertheless, the influence of prestigious institutions on higher education and on the students who join the nation's cultural elite is enormous.

[9] Ibid., pp. 36, 53-54.

[10] Ibid., pp. 13-17, 20.

[11] Information about this and other colleges mentioned here is taken from John Zmirak, ed., *Choosing the Right College 2014-15* (Wilmington, Del.: Intercollegiate Studies Institute, 2013).

[12] George Roche, *The Fall of the Ivory Tower: Government Funding, Corruption, and the Bankrupting of American Higher Education* (Washington, D.C.: Regnery, 1994).

[13] *Imprimis* is available gratis at http://imprimis.hillsdale.edu.

[14] Quoted in Sykes and Miner, p. 61.

[15] See Patrick Riley, "College Accreditation: The Resurgence of Academic Excellence," *Alternatives in Philanthropy*, October 1996, pp. 2-6, which details the politically correct shifts in regional accreditation standards. In addition to the account of Thomas Aquinas, Riley also describes confrontations with Baruch College in New York and Westminster Theological Seminary in Pennsylvania.

[16] http://www.aale.org/.

Chapter X. Myths and Realities

[1] Benedict Ashley and Pierre Conway, "The Liberal Arts in St. Thomas Aquinas," *The Thomist* vol. 22, no. 4, Oct. 1959.

Index

Acknowledgements

The primary credit for this book belongs to the pioneers of the classical renewal: the teachers, headmasters, board members, parents, and students who are experimenting boldly with an education that is both very old and yet very new. Starting a school is a heroic task, and the founders of the schools discussed here—and the many more that are currently being organized and will be organized—are worthy of honor.

In the course of our research, we continually encountered teachers and schools that deserve to be highlighted, and it is certain that many have been left out. In this third edition, we have had to revise nearly every chapter—most notably, those addressing the "elements" of classical education, home-schooling, and higher education. We regret our omissions and emphasize that many more success stories exist than we could mention here.

As with any major project, many minds and hands were involved. We would like to offer special thanks to Peter Vande Brake, Buck Holler, and Edward Chandler for their significant research help. Thanks to Graeme Pitman and David Kern for their work on cover design, and to Scott Walter for his manuscript review.

We also thank those who were willing to be interviewed, e-mailed, called, and questioned, so we could complete this updated edition.

Finally, and above all, we thank our families for their patience and support over the course of this project.

About the Authors

Gene Edward Veith, Jr. has written over 20 books on topics involving Christianity and culture, classical education, literature, and the arts. His books include *God at Work: Your Christian Vocation in All of Life; The Soul of the Lion, the Witch, and the Wardrobe; Reading Between the Lines: A Christian Guide to Literature; State of the Arts: From Bezalel to Mapplethorpe; Painters of Faith: The Spiritual Landscape in 19th Century America; Loving God with All Your Mind; and Postmodern Times: A Christian Guide to Contemporary Thought and Culture.*

Dr. Veith is professor of literature at Patrick Henry College, where he has also served as provost and interim president. He previously served as professor of English and dean of the School of Arts and Sciences at Concordia University Wisconsin, and as the culture editor of World magazine.

Dr. Veith and his wife, Jackquelyn, have three grown children and 11 grandchildren.

Andrew Kern is founder and president of the CiRCE Institute, the founding author of *The Lost Tools of Writing*, and is on the board of the Society for Classical Learning. Since establishing CiRCE as a research and consulting service to classical educators, Andrew has trained teachers, led board retreats, and assisted with institutional development and start up in over 100 schools since 1996. He has directed the CiRCE Institute full time since the summer of 2000.

Andrew helped start Providence Academy in Green Bay, Wisconsin, in 1993, where he served as "Lead Teacher"; Foundations Academy (now Ambrose School) in Boise, Idaho, where he served as director of classical instruction from 1996-2000; the Great Ideas Academy in Charlotte, North Carolina, where he served as headmaster from 2001-2003; and the Regent Schools of the Carolinas, where he served as dean of academics from 2006-2008. He and his family live in North Carolina.

Brian Phillips is the headmaster of the CiRCE Academy and director of CiRCE Consulting, in addition to writing a regular column for the CiRCE Institute. Brian has served as a head of Rhetoric School and as a teacher of humanities, rhetoric, and Latin. He is the pastor of Holy Trinity Reformed Church in Concord, North Carolina; a board member of the Cabarrus Women's Center; an adjust faculty member at Belmont Abbey College; and the author of *Sunday Mornings: An Introduction to Biblical Worship*. He has an M.A. in theological studies and an Ed.D. in humanities and classical education. Brian and his wife, Shannon, have four children.

About the Capital Research Center

The CAPITAL RESEARCH CENTER is a think tank in Washington, D.C., that specializes in the study of civil society. We publish research on public charities, foundations, labor unions, and political activists as part of our mission to educate donors, policymakers, and the news media on the best ways to achieve a free and prosperous society.

America's exceptional freedoms are a result of her Founders' belief in the need to counterbalance government with a strong civil society. Education is a critical ingredient in the project, as Thomas Jefferson explained when he warned, "If a nation expects to be ignorant and free … it expects what never was and never will be." And so we are proud to publish our third edition of this guide to classical education.

For more information on our research, please visit CapitalResearch.org or contact us at

Capital Research Center
1513 Sixteenth Street, NW
Washington, DC 20036
202.483.6900
contact@CapitalResearch.org

How to Order

Capital Research Center's books are published in cooperation with the AmP Publishers Group, whose website offers a 20% discount. Please visit AmPPubGroup.com.

Bulk sales (10 or more copies) are available at a 50% discount. For inquiries, please e-mail info@AmPPubGroup.com or contact their offices at

Sales and Distribution Office
AmP Publishers Group
18 N. Church St., Suite 2
West Chester, PA 19380
302.635.7354
Fax 302.635.7355

AmP Publishers Group books are sold to the trade by the University of Chicago Press. Bookstore buyers and wholesalers should contact:

John Kessler, Sales Director
University of Chicago Press
1427 E. 60th Street
Chicago, IL 60637-2954
773.702.7248
Fax 773.702.9756